History

THE MAKING OF
THE UK 1485–1750

FOR
COMMON
ENTRANCE

History

THE MAKING OF THE UK 1485–1750

FOR COMMON ENTRANCE

N.R.R. Oulton

Subject Editor: Niall Murphy

GALORE PARK

AN HACHETTE UK COMPANY

The Publishers would like to thank the following for permission to reproduce copyright material:

Photo credits: Cover © Classic Image / Alamy **pxiii** © Elmtree Images / Alamy **pxiv** © Bildarchiv Monheim GmbH / Alamy **pxv** © Henry A. Payne/The Bridgeman Art Library/Getty Images **pxviii** © Image Asset Management Ltd. / Alamy **p1** © The Bridgeman Art Library/Getty Images **p3** © TopFoto **p6** © Mary Evans Picture Library / Alamy **p9** © The Bridgeman Art Library/Getty Images **p11** (t) © The Bridgeman Art Library/Getty Images **p11** (b) Portrait of Thomas Wolsey (c.1475-1530) (oil on panel), Strong, Sampson (c.1550-1611) / © Magdalen College, Oxford, UK / The Bridgeman Art Library **p14** © PAINTING / Alamy **p17** © De Agostini Picture Library/Getty Images **p18** © Art Directors & TRIP / Alamy **p23** © Tom Taylor / Alamy **p28** © Photos.com - Thinkstock **p29** © FineArt / Alamy **p31** © Mary Evans Picture Library / Alamy **p32** Edward VI, c.1546 (oil on panel), Scrots, Guillaume (fl.1537-53) (attr. to) / The Royal Collection © 2014 Her Majesty Queen Elizabeth II / The Bridgeman Art Library **p35** © The Bridgeman Art Library/Getty Images **p37** © The Bridgeman Art Library/Getty Images **p39** © Image Asset Management Ltd. / Alamy **p42** © Mary Evans Picture Library / Alamy **p44** The account of the three Guernsey martyrs burned at the stake, from an edition of 'Acts and Monuments' by John Foxe (1516-87) (engraving), English School / © Private Collection / The Bridgeman Art Library **p46** © The Art Gallery Collection / Alamy **p51** © The Bridgeman Art Library/Getty Images **p53** © Fine Art Photographic Library/ Corbis **p60** © The Art Gallery Collection / Alamy **p63** © Image Asset Management Ltd. / Alamy **p71** © 2005 Fotomas / TopFoto **p74** © gilbertdestoke - Fotolia **p76** © Buyenlarge/Getty Images **p78** © British Library/Robana/Getty Images **p79** © DeAgostini/Getty Images **p81** © The Bridgeman Art Library/ Getty Images **p84** © Lebrecht Music and Arts Photo Library / Alamy **p85** (m) © SOTK2011 / Alamy **p85** (b) © Lebrecht Music and Arts Photo Library / Alamy **p86** © SuperStock/Getty Images **p88** © Photos.com - Thinkstock **p93** © 2003 Topham Picturepoint / TopFoto **p98** © The Gallery Collection/Corbis **p101** (t) © J Orr / Alamy **p101** (b) © Nikreates / Alamy **p104** © Robert Walker/The Bridgeman Art Library/Getty Images **p108** © The Art Gallery Collection / Alamy **p111** © 2003 Fotomas / Topham Picturepoint / TopFoto **p114** The Family of Henry Chorley, Haberdasher of Preston, c.1680 (oil on canvas), English School, (17th century) / © Harris Museum and Art Gallery, Preston, Lancashire, UK / The Bridgeman Art Library **p115** © Rudi Tapper/iStock - Thinkstock **p117** The Restoration of Charles II (1630-85) at Whitehall on 29 May 1660, c.1660 (oil on canvas), Fuller, Isaac (1606-72) / © Private Collection / The Bridgeman Art Library **p118** © Image Asset Management Ltd. / Alamy **p121** © The Print Collector / Alamy **p124** © The Bridgeman Art Library/Getty Images **p129** © 2001 Topham Picturepoint / TopFoto **p131** © The Print Collector/Getty Images **p133** (m) George Clifford, 3rd Earl of Cumberland, Hilliard, Nicholas (1547-1619) / Private Collection / Photo © Christie's Images / The Bridgeman Art Library **p133** (b) © Artmedia / HIP / TopFoto **p135** (t) © Photos. com - Thinkstock **p135** (b) Halley enquiring of Newton (gouache on paper), Nicolle, Pat (Patrick) (1907-95) / Private Collection / © Look and Learn / The Bridgeman Art Library **p137** © Mary Evans Picture Library / Alamy **p140** (t) © Articles of Union between England and Scotland from the House of Lords record office, 1707 / © Houses of Parliament, Westminster, London, UK / The Bridgeman Art Library **p140** (m) © The Print Collector / Heritage Images / TopFoto **p141** (t) © John Wootton/The Bridgeman Art Library/Getty Images **p141** (b) © 2010 Mary Evans Picture Library **p146** © Image Asset Management Ltd. / Alamy **p148** © Heritage Image Partnership Ltd / Alamy **p150** King George II (1683-1760) at the Battle of Dettingen, with the Duke of Cumberland and Robert, 4th Earl of Holderness, 27th June 1743, c.1743 (oil on canvas), Wootton, John (1682-1765) / © National Army Museum, London / Acquired with assistance of National Art Collections Fund / The Bridgeman Art Library **p157** © 2010 Mary Evans Picture Library **p158** © GL Archive / Alamy

Acknowledgements: p123 © 2014 The President and Fellows of Harvard College

Every effort has been made to trace all copyright holders, but if any have been inadvertently overlooked the Publishers will be pleased to make the necessary arrangements at the first opportunity.

Although every effort has been made to ensure that website addresses are correct at time of going to press, Galore Park cannot be held responsible for the content of any website mentioned in this book. It is sometimes possible to find a relocated web page by typing in the address of the home page for a website in the URL window of your browser.

Hachette UK's policy is to use papers that are natural, renewable and recyclable products and made from wood grown in sustainable forests.

The logging and manufacturing processes are expected to conform to the environmental regulations of the country of origin.

Orders: please contact Bookpoint Ltd, 130 Milton Park, Abingdon, Oxon OX14 4SB. Telephone: +44 (0)1235 827827. Lines are open 9.00a.m.–5.00p.m., Monday to Saturday, with a 24-hour message answering service. Visit our website at www.galorepark.co.uk for details of other revision guides for Common Entrance, examination papers and Galore Park publications.

Published by Galore Park Publishing Ltd,
An Hachette UK Company
Carmelite House, 50 Victoria Embankment, London EC4Y 0DZ
www.galorepark.co.uk

Text copyright © N.R.R Oulton and Bob Pace 2014

The right of N.R.R. Oulton and Bob Pace to be identified as the authors of this work has been asserted by them in accordance with sections 77 and 78 of the Copyright, Designs and Patents Act 1988.

First edition published 2009
This edition:
Impression number   10 9 8 7 6
2022 2021 2020 2019

Typeset in 10/12 pt ITC Officina Sans Std Book by Integra Software Services Pvt. Ltd., Pondicherry, India
Illustrations by DC Graphic Design Limited, Oxford Designer, and Illustrators Ltd, Ian Douglass and Emmanuel Cerisier
Printed in Dubai

A catalogue record for this title is available from the British Library

ISBN: 978 1 471808 90 6

About the author

Nicholas Oulton read History at Oriel College, Oxford and taught for ten years in both prep and senior schools before setting up Galore Park in 1998.

Notes on features in this book

Words printed in **blue and bold** are keywords. All keywords are defined in the glossary on page 165.

Passages printed in blue and italic are quotations from historical sources. You can read the text before and after each passage to understand where the passage comes from, when it was written and who wrote it.

In the margin you will occasionally find a purple box containing an activity or a suggested topic for you to research. These are optional but will enrich your understanding of this historical period.

Contents

Introduction

A changing world

The period of British History from 1485 to 1750 is a tale of great upheaval in our island story. We will read in this book of wars, rebellions and religious persecution. We will learn how King Charles I was executed by his people, and how, eleven years later, his son was restored to the throne – our republican experiment at an end. We will read about great personalities who have shaped our history for better or worse. This is the age of Henry VIII and his six wives, of Bloody Mary, of Guy Fawkes and of Shakespeare. We will see how the landscape started to be transformed as towns grew and the old feudal order that we learnt about in *History for Common Entrance: Medieval Realms Britain 1066–1485* came to be challenged by a world revolving around trade. And we will see the first beginnings of what was to become a great empire, as Britain looked beyond its own island shores, not to France, as in the past, but to a distant world beyond, in India and America.

Feudal England

Our story opens with a battle that saw England almost tear itself apart as the old order was turned, briefly, on its head. England in 1485 was still, on the whole, a feudal country, but this system was in decline. Its wealth derived from the land, where the vast majority of its people lived and worked. The way to riches lay through the ownership of land, which technically belonged to the king, but much of which in practice was held through a complicated series of feudal relationships by his subjects (nobles and gentry) and by the Church. In return for land, these subjects promised a range of services to the king; to fight for the king in time of war, to obey him at all times, and to maintain the land in good repair. And they also promised to pay a share of the produce derived from the land that they held. They held the land, in effect, at the king's pleasure, and as a result, they had to obey him if they wanted to continue to hold the land.

So, at the top of this system was the king, who owned all the land in his kingdom. To bind his subjects to him, and to secure their support, he granted land to the leading families, the nobles, in return for their loyalty and obedience, their support in time of war and a guarantee of revenue from the land. These nobles, in turn, granted (or gave) portions of the land that they held to lesser men, the gentry, again in return for revenue and service. Obliged to raise an army of men to help defend the king in time of trouble, the nobles needed to secure the support of the men around them who would make up this army. So, they granted land to them in return for a promise of loyalty, a share of the revenues from the land, and an obligation to fight if necessary. These gentry in turn found it necessary to secure the loyalty of the men below them, and they too granted land in exchange for revenue and service.

This system is known as the Feudal System. The person granting the land was the lord; the person he granted the land to was the vassal. The receiving of land by the vassal from the lord was accompanied by an oath of loyalty or fealty in a ceremony known as an act of homage. The vassal paid homage to his lord in return for land.

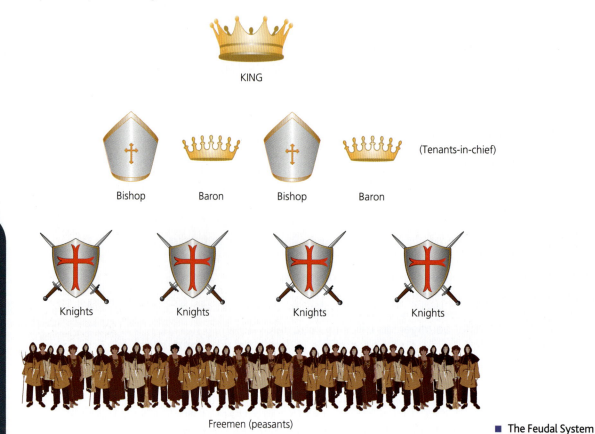

KING

Bishop   Baron   Bishop   Baron   (Tenants-in-chief)

Knights   Knights   Knights   Knights

Freemen (peasants)

■ The Feudal System

The result was a pyramid with the king at the top. Under the king was a group of nobles, his vassals, usually referred to as his tenants-in-chief, and which probably represented between 50 and 100 families. Included among these tenants-in-chief were leading churchmen, abbots, bishops and archbishops, who held land from the king in the same way that dukes and earls did. These tenants-in-chief then had vassals of their own, knights, esquires and lesser churchmen, and then below them were the vast majority of the people, probably around 80–90 per cent of the population. Most of these people lived on the land as peasant farmers, owing their livelihood to their lords and masters higher up the pyramid.

In such a system, in which land was transferred from father to son, and with it, the feudal ties and obligations, there was little room for social mobility. The nobles, by and large, stayed noble; the poor stayed poor. Those who had the king's favour were keen to keep it, with all the wealth and status that this brought.

Trade and the growth of Parliament

Gradually, however, this system began to change. People realised that they could make money, not from the land but by manufacturing things or by trading goods from one place to another. The people who made money in this way were called merchants, and some of these merchants became richer than the nobles. Some even came to have more money than the king himself. Kings and nobles tried to adapt to the new economy by asking their vassals to fulfil their feudal obligations in money rather than in promises of support and, by 1460, the economy of England was probably based on money as much as on services and duties. One of the most important trades was in wool. English wool was famous across Europe for its high quality. Many merchants earned fortunes in wool, and the king taxed the trade to boost his income.

■ A rich merchant's home; Tudor House Museum in Southampton

As these merchants rose in importance economically, so the nobles became less important. However, politically the nobles continued to hold great power. As tenants-in-chief of the king, the nobles were responsible for providing him with counsel (advice) and for upholding law and order. They thus played a vital role in maintaining law and order across the country, presiding over courts and handing out justice. They also took a lead role in government business, and the king was expected to consult them before making any important decisions.

In addition to the counsel provided to the king by the nobles, the idea of a Parliament had begun to develop, with each town or county electing one or more men to attend Parliament to represent that area. In theory, Parliament had the power to agree, or not, to new taxes being imposed on the people by the king. This is what Simon de Montfort and others had fought and died for (see *History for Common Entrance: Medieval Realms Britain 1066–1485*, pages 74–75). Parliament could also debate issues of state, and could humbly ask the king to take action. However, in the end it was the king who decided on new laws and regulations. Parliament might be consulted but it was the king who made the decisions. And critically, as we will see later, it was the king who decided when and for how long Parliament should meet. If the king chose to rule without Parliament, as he often did, it was perfectly possible for him to do so.

The Church

We have already seen that the country's leading churchmen were tenants-in-chief, alongside the leading nobles. The Church at this time was a hugely powerful institution and one of the greatest landowners in the kingdom. Monasteries, convents, bishoprics and other Church organisations held land given to them by the king and owed him services in just the same way as the nobles did. Many clergymen worked in the royal government, aiding the king, and several bishops were invited to councils alongside the noblemen. This was a world in which people – throughout Christendom – looked to

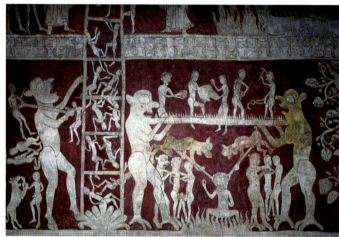

■ A medieval depiction of Hell; a wall-hanging in a church in Surrey made around 1200

the Church for their salvation. Fear of eternal damnation was very real, and without the intervention of the Church on their behalf, they believed they stood no chance of escaping the torments of Hell. Medieval churches were decorated with vivid reminders of this fact for those unable to read or understand the scriptures for themselves. Only with the assistance of the Church, through its bishops and priests, could people, be they kings or peasants, find favour with God.

As a result, kings and nobles, keen to secure their favour with God, were generous to the Church. It is this simple fact that explains the incredible building programme, which saw cathedrals and churches rising up all over Europe during the Middle Ages, and why it was that the Church, as an institution, found itself among the leading landowners of the day. After all, if the Church could secure salvation for those who deserved it, it is hardly surprising that those who could afford to chose to heap gifts on the Church. As we will see when we come to look at the events of Henry VIII's reign, this idea that money could buy salvation came to be challenged. However, as our story opens, it was still a powerful force in society.

Furthermore, the idea that the Church owed its main loyalty, not to the king, as its feudal lord, but to the Pope in Rome, had for hundreds of years been causing upset across Europe. The idea was of course totally at odds with the Feudal System described above and famously led to a conflict between the Holy Roman Emperor and the Pope, called the Investiture Conflict. An uneasy form of compromise existed, with kings and emperors expecting feudal service from all their vassals, including bishops, while these bishops continued to uphold the fact that they were answerable not to these kings and emperors, but to the Pope. This is what lay behind the clash between Henry II and Thomas Becket (see *History for Common Entrance: Medieval Realms Britain 1066–1485,* pages 47–50). As we will see, the matter came to a dramatic head during the reign of Henry VIII.

The Wars of the Roses

This is the background against which we must view the opening of this period: a feudal world, which was beginning, very slowly, to unravel. A world where power lay with those who held land, but increasingly with those who had money and influence. A world in which the king was seen to hold his throne – by right – from God, and yet in which certain powerful people were more than happy to challenge this right. And any sign of weakness on the part of a king was certain to provoke a response from those who thought they might be able to improve their position in society. So it was, in 1454, that when the King, poor old Henry VI, went temporarily insane, a war broke out across England as the leading families struggled for power and ultimately for the throne itself.

■ Yorkists and Lancastrians pick white and red roses; twentieth-century fresco

With the King unable to carry out his royal duties, action had to be taken. Against the wishes of the King's wife, Margaret, a Protector was nominated to rule the land. This was Richard, Duke of York, a distant cousin of the mad king, whose ancestors had been Dukes of York before him. Margaret raised support against Richard and she and her followers became known as Lancastrians, because King Henry and his ancestors were descended from John of Gaunt, a famous Duke of Lancaster.

The conflict between the Yorkists, symbolised by a white rose, and the Lancastrians, symbolised by a red rose, tore England apart. Queen Margaret, fighting for the rights of her husband, demanded that York should give up his powers but York refused. A battle was fought at St Albans in 1455 and King Henry was captured.

Edward IV, 1461–83

Unwilling to give up, in 1460 Margaret raised an army that freed Henry, then marched north to meet York in battle at Wakefield. York was defeated and killed but the war did not end there. Far from it. York's eldest son, Edward, declared to his supporters that he was the rightful king and proclaimed himself King Edward IV. He then led his men into battle once more and defeated Margaret's forces at the Battle of Towton in 1461. King Henry was once more captured and Margaret fled to France. The Battle of Towton was one of the bloodiest battles fought on English soil, with 20 000 killed.

At this stage the plot thickened. Edward, or King Edward IV as he liked to be called, owed much of his support to the hugely powerful Earl of Warwick, the man remembered by history as Warwick 'the Kingmaker'. Sadly for Edward, Warwick chose this moment to change sides, and in 1470 he threw his support behind the exiled Margaret and her husband. However, when Warwick met Edward in battle at the Battle of Barnet in 1471, Warwick was killed and a few weeks later, at the Battle of Tewkesbury, the Lancastrians were again heavily defeated. Edward held the upper hand and when old King Henry died in the Tower of London – possibly poisoned by Edward's younger brother Richard – King Edward IV could at last relax and consider his position as king safe.

Twelve years later, in 1483, Edward died. By then his Yorkist supporters had become powerful throughout the land and he left something which all good kings were supposed to leave: a male heir.

■ King Henry VI dies in the Tower; Edward is safely king

Richard III, 1483–85

Alas, not all stories have happy endings. The new king, Edward V, was only twelve years old and needed someone to rule on his behalf. Enter Richard, Duke of Gloucester, younger brother of Edward IV and the man accused of having poisoned mad old Henry VI in the Tower. Richard was, if nothing else, ambitious, and the prospect of his twelve-year-old nephew being king did not fill him with enthusiasm. Nor did he approve of the behaviour of Elizabeth Woodville, the widow of Edward IV, who quite understandably wished to protect her young son's claim to the throne.

It was therefore extremely good news when the Bishop of Bath and Wells suddenly announced that the marriage between Edward IV and Elizabeth Woodville had been illegal, and that young King Edward V and his brother were illegitimate. Seizing the young princes, Richard whisked them off to the Tower where sadly, but to no one's surprise, they disappeared and were never seen again. Richard then promptly declared himself King Richard III.

Things did not go according to plan for Richard either. A rebellion was immediately raised against him, and the Lancastrians, seemingly defeated at Tewkesbury, rose once more under their most senior noble, Henry Tudor, to challenge the House of York.

⟳ Henry Tudor's claim to the throne

Henry Tudor's claim to the throne was not a strong one. His mother, Lady Margaret Beaufort, was descended from Edward III, but an Act of Parliament passed in the reign of Henry IV had declared members of the Beaufort family illegitimate, barring them from ever claiming the throne. However, Richard III was far from universally popular, and Henry quickly found himself with supporters, not least the King of France, Charles VIII.

Thus it was that, in August 1485, Henry Tudor set off from France with a force of 4000 soldiers and sailed to Milford Haven in Wales, with his uncle Jasper Tudor, the Earl of Pembroke, in support. From there he marched north up the Welsh coast to Aberystwyth, and then went east, gaining backing and soldiers as he went. His main hope of support, however, lay with his stepfather, Lord Thomas Stanley, who, with his brother Sir William Stanley, could offer a substantial force to assist him. The Stanleys were unwilling to commit themselves to Henry until they could be sure of how things would turn out, and they were especially cautious because, at the time, King Richard III was holding Lord Stanley's son hostage!

We can learn about the events of this period from the account of Polydore Vergil. Polydore Vergil was an Italian scholar whose *Anglica Historia* was written on the orders of King Henry VIII some twenty years later. As with all evidence, this has to be treated with caution, especially as we know that it was written on the orders of Henry Tudor's son, a man who clearly wanted to justify the actions of his father and his rightful claim to the throne.

This is how Polydore Vergil recalls the situation:

> *... though Henry was of noble courage, he was in great fear because he thought that he could not assure himself of Thomas Stanley ... Moreover, Henry had heard that King Richard, with an host innumerable, was at hand ... After that he went to Atherstone where he did meet with Thomas and William Stanley ... they discussed tactics should they come to blows with King Richard.*

From this it appears that the Stanleys were certainly contemplating giving their support to Henry, and with this encouragement, Henry decided to risk his luck in battle.

The Battle of Bosworth

Henry Tudor marched at the head of his army and met the forces of King Richard near the village of Market Bosworth in Leicestershire on 22 August 1485. Henry found himself greatly outnumbered, but this was only so if you included the troops controlled by the Stanleys. If the Stanleys were to come over to his side, it would be a very different story.

As the battle closed, Richard III showed his true colours. He identified the part of the battle line where Henry himself was and launched an attack, personally leading the charge. Things looked bad for Henry as his bodyguard fell all around him under the blows of Richard and his men but, at that moment, the Stanleys made their move. Seeing how things were, Sir William Stanley charged across to protect Henry and Richard found himself surrounded. Richard was killed and the battle was won.

As John Rous, a contemporary chronicler, wrote:

This King Richard, who in his time was cruel beyond measure, reigned for a little more than two years, in the way that the Antichrist is to reign ... For all that, let me say the truth to his credit that he bore himself like a soldier and despite his little body and feeble strength, honourably defended himself to his last breath, shouting again and again that he was betrayed and crying 'Treason! Treason! Treason!'

Richard III was the last King of England to die on the battlefield. With his death, a new royal dynasty was ushered in, the Tudors. Henry declared himself King Henry VII and, as if to prove to the world that his claim to the throne was based on more than simply victory in battle, he dated his reign from 21 August, the day before the battle.

■ The Battle of Bosworth; nineteenth-century engraving

Henry VII, 1485–1509

Uniting the kingdom

Henry Tudor came to the throne of England with very little preparation for the role of king. He had spent half his life in exile, mainly in France, and had no experience of government, let alone royal administration. But he knew, perhaps better than those who had gone before him, that to be successful, he had to unite the country around him. That meant, above all else, uniting the Yorkist and Lancastrian factions that had torn the country apart over the previous quarter of a century.

With this in mind, Henry acted quickly to build support. He was crowned on 30 October, and later married, with the Pope's blessing, his own cousin, Elizabeth of York, the daughter of Edward IV and niece of Richard III. At a stroke, the houses of Lancaster and York were reunited, and Henry was firmly at their head.

■ Henry VII; sixteenth-century portrait

Control over the nobility

Henry VII realised that he had to strike a balance between a nobility that was strong enough to help him, and one that might become so powerful that it could threaten his position as king. Henry was fortunate that the Wars of the Roses had seen the deaths of several powerful nobles. He did not create many new nobles to help run the government. Instead, he relied on educated men drawn from the lesser nobility or merchants to serve as officials in return for money or estates.

After the Battle of Bosworth, Henry restored the estates of those Lancastrian nobles who had been stripped of them by Edward IV and Richard III. This included his uncle, Jasper Tudor, the Earl of Pembroke and Duke of Bedford, to whom he was grateful for his support in the years before Bosworth. He also restored land to John de Vere, the Earl of Oxford, and to John Morton, the Bishop of Ely. Some land taken from defeated Yorkists was handed to his supporters, and Thomas Stanley was made Earl of Derby as a reward for his part in the victory. By contrast, high profile Yorkists who had fought against him had their land taken away.

In 1487 Henry reorganised the Court of Star Chamber and increased its power to deal with cases of rebellion, allowing him to clamp down hard on anyone who resisted his rule. He used fines and the confiscation of land from traitors to increase his income. Justices of the Peace were appointed from the gentry to administer justice and to help maintain law and order.

Henry and retaining

Another way in which Henry restricted the potential threat posed by the nobles was to restrict the practice of **retaining**. Under the **Feudal System**, the king's **tenants-in-chief** had been accustomed to keep their own private armies which, in return for the land that they held, they would put at the service of the king in time of trouble. This keeping of private armies was called retaining. Having seen at first hand how much power this gave to the nobles – his own victory at Bosworth had been secured due to the part played by the forces of the Stanley family – Henry decided by the law of livery to restrict retaining, issuing licences which specified exactly how many soldiers a lord could keep and imposing heavy fines on those who broke the agreement. He also forced some nobles to sign a written contract called a **recognisance** by which they agreed to pay a sum of money as a guarantee of their loyalty and good behaviour. If they misbehaved, they were fined.

As we read in the *Anglica Historia* by Polydore Vergil (see page xvii):

Henry wished to keep all Englishmen obedient through fear, and he considered that when they gave him offence they were motivated by their great wealth ... When his subjects who were men of substance were found guilty of whatever fault, he harshly fined them by a penalty which deprived them of their fortunes, not only the men themselves but even their descendants.

Henry's Council

Henry further reduced the political power of the senior nobles by taking away their right to attend his Council. Before this time, the king's tenants-in-chief were entitled to attend his Council, but Henry changed things so that only those whom he invited were entitled to attend. Increasingly Henry relied for advice on those from the gentry, the knights and esquires, and from the growing professional classes and merchants, men who understood the law and the importance of money. Such men were appointed as Justices of the Peace (JPs) and became responsible for keeping order and implementing new laws. Henry used committees made up of such men for specific tasks – to run the Court of Requests, the Court of Star Chamber and a special court to oversee retaining. Furthermore, by re-establishing the Council of the North and the Council of Wales, Henry was able to extend his authority into those regions without the need to rely on the nobles.

So it was that men such as Richard Empson, Edmund Dudley, Edward Poynings and Reginald Bray came to prominence at the expense of the traditional landed nobility. One can see why Henry was not universally popular with the latter.

Justices of the Peace still exist, in some form. By what name are they more commonly known? What sort of things do they deal with today?

⬤ Lambert Simnel, the first pretender

Although Henry was now king, and he may have taken some comfort when his first son, Arthur, was born in 1486, giving him the heir that kings value so highly, Henry was not able to relax. He still had many enemies and the first to raise trouble against him was a priest from Oxford called Richard Symonds.

In 1486, Richard Symonds attempted to pass off one of his pupils, the son of an Oxford baker named Lambert Simnel, as Richard III's nephew Edward, the Earl of Warwick. The young Earl of Warwick was being held by Henry in the Tower of London and Symonds had heard a rumour that he had been murdered. He took Simnel to Ireland where he was warmly welcomed as an

■ Richard Empson, Henry VII and Edmund Dudley; from an anonymous portrait produced in the sixteenth century

alternative to King Henry VII, and before long Simnel – still pretending to be the Earl of Warwick – was crowned 'King Edward VI'. At the time he was no more than ten years old, and although he used the name 'King Edward VI', he was never widely recognised as such, and it was 60 years before England had a real king of that name.

Simnel received support from the sister of Edward IV and from the Earl of Lincoln, under whose leadership a force was raised to challenge for the throne. Their case was made to look a little weak, of course, when Henry VII revealed in public the real Earl of Warwick, alive and well. At the Battle of East Stoke in 1487, Lincoln was defeated and killed. Those who had supported Simnel had their lands confiscated and Symonds was thrown into prison. As for Lambert Simnel, Henry took pity on him and put him to work in his kitchen, and he later became a royal falconer.

In November of that year, eager to calm his Yorkist critics, Henry had his wife, Elizabeth of York, crowned queen. As we have seen, Elizabeth was Richard III's niece, and her coronation was an obvious attempt to placate those still loyal to Richard and the Yorkists.

Exercise 1.1

Read pages xvii–4 and then answer the following questions:

1 How strong was Henry Tudor's claim to the throne of England? Write a few sentences.

2 Suggest reasons why Henry VII:

   (a) dated his reign from the day before the Battle of Bosworth

   (b) married Elizabeth of York

   (c) called his son Arthur.

3 Explain the most serious threats that Henry VII faced during the first part of his reign, and how he dealt with them.

Perkin Warbeck, the second pretender

Having dealt with the challenge posed by Lambert Simnel, Henry soon after faced another pretender to the throne, this time claiming to be Prince Richard, the younger of the two 'Princes in the Tower' allegedly murdered by Richard III. Once more, the pretender went to Ireland and once more, he was welcomed as the true King of England.

The name of this second pretender was Perkin Warbeck. In 1491, Warbeck went to Ireland to raise support, and the next year he went to France and then on to visit Maximilian, the Holy Roman Emperor, who recognised Warbeck as 'King Richard IV'. Henry was obviously keen to disprove Warbeck's claims, and sent spies to find out exactly who he was, and to prove that he was certainly not Prince Richard, as he claimed to be. During this process, Henry found evidence that his old supporter and saviour William Stanley had been plotting with Warbeck, and Stanley was executed.

Warbeck continued to gain support, next from King James IV of Scotland, who married Warbeck to his cousin, Catherine Gordon. But little actually came of the threat he posed, and in 1497 he joined a rebellion in Cornwall, not in support of his cause, but in protest against taxation. The Cornish rebels had marched to London, were defeated at Blackheath, and were now regrouping back in Cornwall. Warbeck hoped to march at the head of a revived rebellion, but he was not a great soldier. When Henry's forces came to deal with the rebels, Warbeck ran away and was soon captured and taken to London.

The tax rebellions

Henry faced his first rebellion against tax in 1489, when he tried to raise a tax to pay for a war against France. In the past, wars against France had been paid for by the southern counties; the northern counties had only paid for wars against Scotland. Taxation was unpopular at the best of times, and many people in Yorkshire refused to pay. When the Earl of Northumberland tried to collect the money for Henry, he was attacked by a mob of protesters and killed. The rebels went on to form a small army but it was soon defeated and most of the ringleaders were hanged at York.

Eight years later, in 1497, Henry faced another rebellion, this time in Cornwall. Once again taxation was the cause of the trouble, and the rebels, with the support of a noble, Lord Audley, marched towards London with a force of around 15 000 men. It was this rebellion that Perkin Warbeck had joined, although as we have seen, his contribution was far from helpful to the rebels.

We can read about the fate of the Cornish rebels in a record held at Oxford, the *Registrum Annalium Collegii Mertonensis*, which records the end of the rebellion in its account for the year 1497:

The rebels reached Blackheath on 16th June and, the next day, Henry VII met them with a great multitude of nobles. He gained the victory without great slaughter on either side and the rebel leaders and Lord Audley were sent to the Tower in chains. The leaders were hanged and their bodies quartered and by the king's orders the quarters were hanged in various cities and places in the kingdom. Lord Audley's head was struck off near the Tower and his body buried in Blackfriars. His head was fixed on London Bridge.

About 1000 rebels were killed and the rest fled. And while Henry had again defeated those who dared to rebel against him, he determined not to become involved again in expensive wars that relied on taxation.

Perkin Warbeck, the end of the story

Perkin Warbeck had been a huge irritant to Henry, and things did not end when he was captured in 1497 during the Cornish Rebellion. Henry had chosen not to punish Warbeck, and indeed kept him at his royal court in a position of favour, although attended by guards. Warbeck, however, grew restless, and tried to escape – so Henry threw him into the Tower of London, where he met up with the Earl of Warwick, the man whom Lambert Simnel had claimed to be. Later, both Warbeck and Warwick were put to death.

1491	Landed in Ireland and claimed to be Richard of York.
1492	Travelled to France and then to Burgundy.
1493	Maximilian, Holy Roman Emperor, recognised Warbeck as Richard IV.
1494–95	Henry's spies arrested William Stanley and executed him when links to Warbeck were discovered.
1495	Moved to Scotland and gained support from James IV.
1496	Married a cousin of James IV. A Scots force led by Warbeck invaded England but failed to win support.
1497	Went to Ireland and then to Cornwall, where he was arrested. Henry kept him and his wife at court.
1498	Escaped custody, was recaptured and imprisoned in the Tower.
1499	Hanged at Tyburn along with the Earl of Warwick.

■ Perkin Warbeck in the pillory

> Look into the stories of Lambert Simnel and Perkin Warbeck. How are they similar and how are they different? Which do you think was the more serious threat to Henry VII's rule?

Foreign policy

As might be understandable from all this, Henry VII spent much of his reign anxious about the security of his throne and his policy overseas was guided by his fear of trouble at home. It was his belief that, if he could bring peace and stability to his kingdom, foreign powers would be less inclined to interfere or to give their support to rebels or pretenders. So, in 1489, shortly after the scare of Lambert Simnel, Henry signed the Treaty of Medina del Campo with Spain, by which Henry agreed to the marriage of his son Arthur and Catherine of Aragon, daughter of King Ferdinand and Queen Isabella of Spain. Three years later he signed the Treaty of Etaples with France, in the same year that the King of France had offered assistance to Perkin Warbeck. Later in his reign, in 1502, he agreed to the marriage of his daughter Margaret to King James IV of Scotland, who had earlier offered assistance to Perkin Warbeck, and in 1508 he betrothed his other daughter, Mary, to the Archduke Charles of Burgundy, a marriage that never took place.

A fear of foreign support for his enemies at home, and a realisation that wars cost money which he could not afford, dictated the foreign policy of Henry VII.

Exercise 1.2

Look at the timeline on page 6 illustrating the career of Perkin Warbeck.

1 Make a flow chart showing the key events in his career.

2 Explain why he was such a threat to Henry VII.

Exercise 1.3

Explain the reasons why Henry VII faced rebellions during his reign.

Henry's death

The death of Perkin Warbeck in 1499 marked the end of Yorkist threats to Henry, but he never felt secure. Between 1500–02, two of his sons, Edmund and Arthur, died, and in 1503 his wife Elizabeth died too. He still had one precious male heir, Henry, who had been born in 1491, but he never felt that his grip on the English throne was secure, or that the new Tudor dynasty was firmly established.

When he died in 1509, the Bishop of Rochester said of Henry VII:

His politic wisdom in governance was singular ... his reason pithy and substantial, his memory fresh and holding, his experience notable, his counsels fortunate and taken by wise deliberation, his speech gracious in various languages.

However, few seemed to mourn Henry. On hearing the news of his death, Sir Thomas More (a Member of Parliament who had resented Henry's taxes and financial penalties) said:

This day is the end of our slavery, the fount of our liberty, the end of sadness, the beginning of joy.

Polydore Vergil, who owed his position in England to Henry VII, wrote the following obituary in *Anglica Historia* about five years after the King's death:

His spirit was distinguished, wise and prudent, his mind was brave, and never, even at moments of the greatest danger, deserted him ... He cherished justice above all things ... but all these virtues were obscured latterly by avarice ... In a monarch it may be considered the worst vice, since it is harmful to everyone.

Exercise 1.4

1 Write a few sentences on the importance during the reign of Henry VII of each of the following:

   (a) Retaining

   (b) Recognisance

   (c) The Council

   (d) The professional classes

2 Explain how successful Henry VII was in controlling the nobility during his reign.

Exercise 1.5

Explain the consequences of Henry VII's foreign policy.

Exercise 1.6

Look back at the whole chapter and, as you are reading it, think about the work of Henry VII. Consider the aims he had. Then copy the table below and fill in the boxes.

Henry VII's reign	
Successes	Failures

2 Henry VIII, 1509–47

◯ A Renaissance prince: Henry's early life

Henry became King of England in 1509, when he was only seventeen years old. He looked every inch a king, standing 6 feet 2 inches (1 m 88 cm) tall at a time when the average height for men was about 5 feet 6 inches (1 m 68 cm); and he was both handsome and athletic.

On his accession, Lord Mountjoy wrote to the philosopher Erasmus about the new King:

I have no fear but when you heard that our Prince, now Henry the Eighth, had succeeded to his father's throne, all your melancholy left you at once. What may you not promise yourself from a Prince with whose extraordinary and almost divine character you are acquainted? When you know what a hero he now shows himself, how wisely he behaves, what a lover he is of justice and goodness, what affection he bears to the learned. If you could see how all the world here is rejoicing in the possession of so great a Prince, how his life is all their desire, you could not contain your tears for joy! Avarice is expelled the country. Our King does not desire gold or gems or precious metals, but virtue, glory, immortality.

■ Henry VIII; from an anonymous portrait produced around 1509

Henry was born at Greenwich on 28 June 1491. He received a sound education and was taught Latin, French, Italian and Spanish. He was good at mathematics and well schooled in theology. Many historians think that his father wanted him to follow a career in the Church. Indeed, the strong emphasis that was placed upon theology and its complex debates remained with Henry for the rest of his life.

However, when his elder brother Arthur died in 1502, all this changed. Henry was created Prince of Wales, and came under the close protection of his anxious father who was keen to preserve his only surviving son. But then, in 1509, his father died and everything changed again. After seven years of being kept away from the world, all of the energy and enthusiasm of Henry's character, which had been restrained since his brother's death, could now be set free.

As a young man, Henry excelled at sport, especially jousting, hunting and royal tennis. In 1513, John Taylor, a diarist, wrote the following about Henry:

Three ambassadors came to the King, who was practising archery in a garden with the archers of his guard. He split the mark in the middle, and surpassed them all, as he surpasses them in stature and personal graces.

Clearly a man of energy, Henry was keen to show his physical prowess at all times. In 1515, Sagudino, secretary to the Venetian ambassador, wrote:

The Queen and twenty-five attendants found the King and his guard in green liveries ... there followed jousting and his majesty looked like St. George on horseback. They jousted for three hours ... the King excelled all others, breaking many lances and unhorsing one of his opponents.

Henry had written many poems and several pieces of music, and having been educated in the ways of the 'new learning' – the Renaissance (rebirth of classical culture with its emphasis on a wide-ranging education) – he came to typify the spirit of the new age. Giustiniani, a Venetian ambassador writing about Henry in 1519, said:

He is athletic and highly intelligent. He speaks good French, Latin and Spanish; is very religious; heard three masses daily ... He is extremely fond of hunting, and never takes that diversion without tiring eight or ten horses ... He is also fond of tennis. He devotes himself to pleasure and ease and leaves the cares of the state to Cardinal Wolsey.

Later in his life, Henry was involved in the construction and improvement of several significant buildings, including Nonsuch Palace, King's College Chapel in Cambridge and Westminster Abbey, as well as the improvement of existing buildings such as Christ Church in Oxford, Hampton Court Palace and the Palace of Whitehall.

> Look into young Prince Henry's education. How typical was this in the sixteenth century? How similar is it to what you learn at school?

Exercise 2.1

1 Look at the painting of young Henry on page 9. Describe the impression of him that you get from this painting.

2 Look at the picture of Henry on page 10. What message do you think Henry and Holbein were trying to convey in this painting? Explain your answer carefully.

3 Write a brief description of the young Henry VIII using the information in this section. To what extent do the two pictures give differing views of the King, and to what extent do they agree?

4 Henry has sometimes been called a 'Renaissance prince'. What is meant by this phrase? Explain whether you think Henry was such a prince.

5 Find out about the careers of the painter Hans Holbein and the writer Erasmus. Write about half a page on each.

Thomas Wolsey

Within five years of Henry becoming king, England became involved in wars against France and Scotland. It was during this period that Henry came to rely on Thomas Wolsey. Wolsey was the son of a wealthy Ipswich tradesman who, after taking his degree at Oxford at the age of fourteen, had become a priest, then risen to become a senior official in the Church, and then moved on to become a royal official. In 1513, he organised the King's forces for an invasion of France and negotiated a peace treaty in 1514. These successes led to his promotion to become Henry's chief minister. He became Lord Chancellor and Archbishop of York, and displayed his status and considerable wealth in his elaborate Hampton Court (later a royal palace).

George Cavendish, a close associate of Wolsey, wrote in 1557 that:

Wolsey had a smooth tongue and ornate eloquence.

However, Polydore Vergil wrote in *Anglica Historia* that Wolsey:

… with his arrogance and ambition, raised against himself the hatred of the whole people and, in his hostility towards nobles and common folk, procured their great irritation at his vainglory. His own odiousness was truly complete, because he claimed he could undertake himself almost all public duties.

Certainly, Henry was content that much of the work of government could be looked after by a close advisor such as Wolsey. The Venetian ambassador wrote in 1519 that Wolsey:

… transacted alone the same business as that which occupied all magistrates, offices and councils of Venice, both civil and criminal; and all state affairs were managed by him.

Wolsey came to dominate the running of the Church and government in England for fifteen years and during his time as Henry's chief advisor, Wolsey was often called *alter rex* (the 'other king').

■ Henry VIII, from a portrait by Hans Holbein the Younger c.1537

> Hampton Court is well worth a visit. If you can go, try to get a sense of how rich and powerful Wolsey had become at the time of its building. Is it significant that it later became a royal palace?

■ Thomas Wolsey; from a portrait by Sampson Strong c. 1550–1611

Wolsey and finance

In order to finance Henry's ambitions to have both a sumptuous Renaissance court at home and a successful foreign policy, Wolsey had to raise large amounts of money. Henry had been keen to show that the unpopular ways of his father were at an end, and one of the first acts of his reign was to execute the unpopular finance ministers, Richard Empson and Edmund Dudley (see page 3). Assisted by the Treasurer of the Chamber, Sir John Heron, Wolsey now devised a tax called the **subsidy**, which sought to place an accurate valuation on each taxpayer's wealth and was considered a fairer approach to taxation than the methods which had preceded it. However, he also continued Henry VII's policy of forcibly obtaining money from the nobility by the use of compulsory gifts to the Crown, known as **benevolences**, and in 1522 these gifts alone raised over £200 000 for the King. Less successful was Wolsey's attempt to raise money for war in 1525 using a non-parliamentary tax known as the **Amicable Grant**. So unpopular was this that open revolt was threatened and Wolsey abandoned it.

Enclosures and legal redress

A process during Henry's reign which continued to cause resentment was **enclosure**, the fencing off of land which had previously been open for the use of all. Under the Feudal System, land was held from the lord in return for an agreed level of service or payment. Strips of land were held by peasant farmers, which they worked alongside one another, season by season. In addition to the land they held from the lord, areas of **common land** in and around the villages were used by all to graze animals and to provide firewood. Enclosure ended all that. Common land, formerly available for all in the village, was fenced off by the lord, and the villagers' sheep and goats were turned off the land. At the same time, many landowners turned from arable farming to sheep farming, which allowed them to benefit from the profitable wool trade. Sheep farming was much less labour intensive than arable farming and led landowners to enclose the fields, which previously had been divided up into strips for the peasants to work on.

All of this caused much hardship among the peasants who had relied on their rights over the common land to supplement their meagre earnings. When the land was taken away, some fought back by tearing down the walls and fences, and rising up in mobs to challenge or even kill the lords. Others simply gave up and moved away from the land of their ancestors, heading instead for the towns.

Although Wolsey is often seen as power hungry, he was also considered a man with a keen sense of natural justice. The hardships caused by enclosures concerned him, and he carried out enquiries into illegal enclosure in 1517, 1518 and 1526, which led to prosecution for those landowners who had enclosed land without proper permission.

Wolsey also re-established the position of the Court of Star Chamber and the Court of Chancery, in both of which cases could be heard inexpensively and justice could be handed out impartially, away from the domineering control of the nobility. He also re-established the Court of Requests for the poor, where cases could be heard free of charge. So popular were these legal reforms that, in some areas, overflow courts were required to deal with the demand.

Wolsey and the Church

Another area Wolsey devoted himself to was the Church. Wolsey was appointed the Pope's legate in 1518 and, as such, was one of the most powerful churchmen in England. Although possessing huge wealth himself, and guilty of clerical offences such as holding more than one bishopric and failing to visit his dioceses regularly, Wolsey nonetheless made efforts to stamp out abuse in the Church. Corruption was rife throughout the Church, and he used his powers as legate to close down 30 of the most corrupt monasteries, diverting the revenues from these to found a grammar school in Ipswich and a college in Oxford: Cardinal College (which later became Christ Church).

Wolsey and foreign policy

The foreign policy favoured by Wolsey (though not necessarily by Henry) was simple: he wanted to raise the profile and importance in Europe of England and Henry, while avoiding expensive wars. At this time, the three main powers in Europe were France, Spain and the Holy Roman Empire. These powers in turn were all dependent on peaceful relations with the Pope. The King of France was Francis I, and the King of Spain was Charles I. Importantly, Charles I was, from 1519, also the Holy Roman Emperor Charles V, which meant that he controlled most of what is now Germany, parts of Italy and eastern Europe, as well as his own kingdom of Spain. Charles V (as we will call him) was the nephew of Henry VIII's wife, Catherine of Aragon, and so was considered a natural ally of Henry's.

Wolsey was determined to establish peaceful relations with all the major powers of Europe and in 1518 brought together at the Treaty of London the Papacy, together with the rulers of France, Spain, the Holy Roman Empire, Burgundy and the

■ Europe in the early sixteenth century

Netherlands. The powers all signed a treaty of non-aggression, and a marriage was arranged between Henry's daughter Mary and Francis, the son of King Francis of France. After the treaty had been signed, the Venetian ambassador said of Wolsey:

Nothing pleases him more than to be called the arbiter of Christendom.

The Field of the Cloth of Gold

Wolsey next arranged a meeting of Henry and Francis near Calais on 7 June 1520, which has come to be known as the 'Field of the Cloth of Gold'. Both monarchs had hoped to become the Holy Roman Emperor on the death of the Emperor Maximilian, and when Maximilian's grandson Charles V was elected instead, Henry and Francis met to decide what they should do. Henry sent hundreds of craftsmen to build a wooden palace, which was then gilded. Inside the palace, golden tapestries and embroideries decorated the walls. Francis had a huge tent built with a roof of golden cloth. There were nearly three weeks of festivities as each monarch tried to outdo the other in splendour.

■ The Field of the Cloth of Gold in 1520; a sixteenth-century painting

The meeting of the two kings was a fantastic spectacle, and led to the signing of a treaty of friendship, but as the Venetian ambassador who witnessed the events noted:

These sovereigns are not at peace. They hate each other cordially.

Indeed, despite the treaty, Wolsey was prepared to go to war with France as soon as 1523. However, this war led to nothing and Wolsey sought peace again in 1526 to avoid any further expense.

The Church before the Reformation

The Church held an important place in the life of people living in England at this time, and its priests were often hard-working and diligent men. However, as we noted above, there was corruption and bad practice, and not everyone approved of the way the Church was run.

Pluralism was one problem which caused resentment. Many bishops and priests (such as Wolsey) had become rich by holding more than one office at the same time, paying other, often ill-educated, men to carry out their duties while taking the majority of the income from the post for themselves. Some of these men were illiterate and totally unsuited to conducting church services. Not only did this lead to a situation where the work of the Church was not being carried out properly; it also led to great wealth being accumulated in the hands of certain members of the clergy, and this caused resentment. People saw monasteries and bishoprics controlling vast amounts of land and earning huge revenues, and began to question whether this money should not be spent on looking after the poor, rather than on building lavish palaces and funding luxurious lifestyles for abbots and bishops.

People also began to question the precise role of priests. Church services were conducted in Latin and the Bible was generally only available in Latin. The role of the priests was to act as intermediaries between the people and God. However, at around this time a few very well-educated clerics started to believe that people ought to be able to build their own relationship with God, and to read the Bible for themselves, rather than relying solely on the priests to do this for them.

Some priests were sympathetic to these ideas, and wanted to reform the Church, but many bitterly opposed any change, particularly where it threatened to reduce their power and influence.

Martin Luther

The process of criticism reached a turning point in 1517. Martin Luther, a German monk and theologian, made a list of ninety-five points (the 'Ninety-Five Theses') outlining the problems with the Church and nailed this to the door of a church in Wittenberg in Germany. His most important criticism concerned the way in which people were able to buy indulgences.

To understand what an indulgence was, we first need to understand the idea of Purgatory. Catholics believed that, after death, one's soul went to a place called Purgatory, where it was purged or cleansed of all its worldly faults. If this process was successful, the soul passed on to Heaven; if not, the soul went to Hell. To speed up the process, and to ensure that it was successful, it was believed that people were able to ask the Church to intervene on their behalf, by saying prayers for them and, importantly, by granting them an indulgence.

What Luther objected to was the fact that the Church was *selling* these indulgences, and this led him to question the very idea that lay behind them.

As Luther developed his ideas, others joined in the debate that he had started. The movement became known as **Protestantism**, because Luther and his followers protested against the current teachings of the Church. The Catholic Church taught that priests mediated between people and God and that the Pope was God's chief representative on Earth. Luther believed that it was up to individuals to find their own relationship with God, rather than relying on the intervention of priests. This was why he wanted the Bible translated into languages that ordinary people could understand.

Catholics also believed that saints could intervene on their behalf and help them get to heaven. Praying to saints, therefore, was an important part of a Catholic's religion, and the Church exploited this by charging money to people who wanted to pray at places associated with saints, especially where **relics** of saints were held. (Relics were remains of saints, such as pieces of bone or clothing, which were often preserved in churches.) Protestants believed that the relics of the saints were just that, relics, which had no place in the relationship between man and God.

Another key element in the dispute between Catholics and Protestants concerned the bread and wine used in church services. Roman Catholics believed that during the **Eucharist** (communion service), the consecrated bread was transformed into the actual body of Christ, and the wine into the blood of Christ, a process called **transubstantiation**. Protestants disputed this, and many claimed that the bread simply represented and commemorated his body, while the wine commemorated his blood.

In the face of the mounting criticism of the Church, Henry wrote a book attacking Luther and defending the Roman Catholic Church. As a result, in 1521, he and his successors were awarded the title *Fidei Defensor* (Defender of the Faith) by the Pope. If you look at a British coin, you will see that the present monarch continues to hold this title. Look for the letters FD. Henry's good relationship with the Pope was not to last, however.

The King's Great Matter

Henry VIII is perhaps best known for the fact that he had six wives. His first wife was Catherine of Aragon, whom he married in 1509.

As we saw on page 6, Catherine had previously been married to Henry's elder brother Arthur in 1501, as part of a treaty of friendship between England and Spain, but Arthur had died just four months after the wedding. Henry VII had then suggested that his younger son, Henry, should marry Catherine when he was old enough. The marriage was agreed only after the Pope had granted Henry and Catherine **dispensation**, or special permission, to marry, as marrying one's brother's widow was against the rules of the Church.

We have already learnt that one of the primary objectives of a king was to secure his succession by producing at least one male heir, preferably several. We know this had been a source of concern to Henry VII, even though he had a healthy son on his death. By the late 1520s, Henry VIII was also becoming worried as he was yet to father a male heir to the throne. He had a daughter Mary, but he needed a son. His wife Catherine was unlikely to produce any more children. England had once experimented with a female ruler, when the Empress Matilda had attempted to be made queen in the twelfth century, but it was not a precedent that Henry wished to follow.

■ Catherine of Aragon; sixteenth-century portrait

Henry eventually questioned why he was unable to produce a son, and began to believe that he was being punished by God for marrying his brother's widow. He quoted the Bible to support his fears:

> *If a man shall take his brother's wife it is an unclean thing ... they shall be childless.*

Leviticus 20:21

Some people at the time countered Henry's claim by quoting from another part of the Bible, the book of Deuteronomy:

> *If brethren dwell together, and one of them die, and have no child, the wife of the dead shall not marry unto a stranger: her husband's brother shall go unto her, and take her to him to wife ...*

Deuteronomy 25:5

But Henry's mind was made up. He needed a son, and the only way to achieve that was to end his marriage to Catherine and find a new wife capable of bearing a son. To do this, Henry needed an **annulment** stating that his marriage to Catherine had been illegal and therefore, in the eyes of the Church, had never happened. As this issue developed, it became known as the 'King's Great Matter'.

Opposition to the annulment

Catherine of Aragon was unwilling to divorce Henry, and the King needed help from the Pope to achieve his wishes. However, this was a problem because the Pope at that time, Clement VII, was (since the Sack of Rome in 1527) being held virtually as a prisoner by Catherine's

> The issue of whether women are fit to rule occurs again and again throughout history. Empress Matilda is one example: can you find any more? Has recent history anything to tell us on this issue?

nephew, the Holy Roman Emperor Charles V. Charles obviously opposed Henry's plans to remove Catherine from the English throne, and the Pope was unable to go against Charles's wishes.

Pressure to achieve Henry's break with Catherine mounted when he fell in love with a striking young lady at his court, Anne Boleyn. Henry had previously had an affair with Anne's elder sister Mary, but it was Anne who seems to have captivated him. As the Venetian ambassador Savorgnano wrote in the early 1530s, Anne was 'a young woman of noble birth, though many say of bad character, whose will is law to him, and he is expected to marry her should the divorce take place'. Letters between Henry and Anne survive which show the strength of his feelings for her. Here are a few extracts:

> *My mistress and friend: I and my heart put ourselves in your hands, begging you to have them suitors for your good favour, and that your affection for them should not grow less through absence.*
>
> *I beseech you now, with the greatest earnestness, to let me know your whole intention as to the love between us two. I must of necessity obtain this answer from you, having been for a whole year struck with the dart of love.*
>
> *No more to you at this present mine own darling for lack of time but that I would you were in my arms or I in yours for I think it long since I kissed you.*

■ Henry VIII dismisses Cardinal Wolsey from court; from a children's history book published in 1905

Eager to marry Anne, and to produce the son he so badly needed, Henry turned to Wolsey to bring things to a conclusion. Wolsey, as a cardinal and papal legate, was well placed to bring influence to bear on the Pope, and in 1529 Clement VII sent Cardinal Campeggio to England to hear Henry's case. A special court was held at Blackfriars at which Catherine declared that her marriage to Henry was valid. The court failed to reach a conclusion and Pope Clement said that the case would need to be heard by him in Rome. Henry realised that he – or rather Wolsey – had failed.

The fall of Wolsey

Henry was bitterly disappointed by his failure to secure an annulment for his marriage to Catherine, and blamed Wolsey. Those at court sensed the growing rift between the two, and began to attack him. Henry dismissed Wolsey from most of his posts, and Wolsey retired to York, where he was allowed to remain as

Archbishop. It was his first visit to the city! However, when his enemies discovered that he had written to the Pope begging him not to allow Henry to marry Anne, Wolsey was finished. He was summoned to London on charges of treason, but died of stomach cancer in 1530 on the journey south, a broken man. His last words were, 'I wish I had served God as diligently as I served my King.'

The annulment

After Wolsey's death, Henry still hoped that the Pope might be persuaded to grant an annulment. Then, late in 1532, Anne Boleyn became pregnant. Henry was convinced that Anne would bear him a son and he therefore needed to marry her as soon as possible.

Henry had by this time appointed a new Archbishop of Canterbury, Thomas Cranmer, a Protestant who had already spoken out in favour of the annulment. Cranmer married Henry and Anne at a secret ceremony in January 1533. Then, in May, he annulled Henry's marriage to Catherine, allowing Henry to have Anne crowned as queen in a sumptuous ceremony.

As the Tudor chronicler Edward Hall wrote:

On 1st June Queen Anne was brought from Westminster Hall to St Peter's Abbey in procession, with all the monks of Westminster going in rich copes of gold, with thirteen mitred abbots; and after them all the king's chapel in rich copes with four bishops and two mitred archbishops, and all the lords going in their Parliament robes, and the crown borne before her by the duke of Suffolk, and her two sceptres by two earls, and she herself going under a rich canopy of cloth of gold, dressed in a kirtle of crimson velvet decorated with ermine, and a robe of purple velvet decorated with ermine over that, and a rich coronet with a cap of pearls and stones on her head ...

And so she was brought to St Peter's church at Westminster, and there set in her high royal seat, which was made on a high platform before the altar. And there she was anointed and crowned queen of England by the archbishop of Canterbury and the archbishop of York.

The Pope was outraged, and **excommunicated** Henry, claiming that his behaviour had offended God and the Church. Excommunication was an extremely serious punishment, because it prevented Henry from taking part in church services and effectively cut him off from the Church. As it was only through the intervention of priests that one could secure salvation, excommunication effectively ended Henry's hopes of getting to Heaven. However, Henry had started to believe that he himself should be head of the Church in England, which would have meant that the Pope's views did not concern him.

In September of 1533, Anne gave birth; but to Henry's horror, not to the longed-for son, but to a daughter, Elizabeth.

Thomas Cromwell and the Reformation Parliament

In 1529, while Henry had been waiting for the annulment, Parliament had been called. Henry wanted help in his dealings with the Pope and he turned to his new chief advisor, Thomas Cromwell, to achieve his aims. Cromwell had Protestant sympathies, and was a reformer who wished to reduce the power of the Pope in England. He was therefore the ideal man to manage the break with Rome on Henry's behalf. Cromwell was born in 1485 of humble origins, but had studied law and risen to prominence while working with Wolsey, assisting him with the dissolution of the most corrupt monasteries (see page 13). Henry was greatly impressed with Cromwell and gave him important administrative jobs, including Chancellor of the Exchequer and the posts of King's Secretary and Lord Privy Seal.

Under Cromwell's careful handling, what has become known as the 'Reformation Parliament' passed a series of acts cutting back papal power and influence in England.

Acts of the Reformation Parliament		
1532	Act in Restraint of Annates	This stopped all payments to the Pope from the English Church.
1533	Act in Restraint of Appeals	This forbade appeals to Rome, stating that England was an empire governed by one supreme head and king who possessed 'whole and entire' authority within the realm, and that no judgements or excommunications from Rome were valid. It prevented Catherine of Aragon from appealing to the Pope.
1533	Act of Succession	This declared the marriage to Catherine of Aragon to have been unlawful, rendering Princess Mary illegitimate. It stated that the heirs to the throne would be the children of Henry and Anne Boleyn.
1534	Act of Supremacy	This made Henry the head of the English Church instead of the Pope.
1534	Treason Act	This meant that anyone who denied Henry's position as head of the Church could be tried for treason.
1534	Act for First Fruits and Tenths	This permitted Henry to take the first year's revenue from all bishoprics and benefices. All clerics then had to pay one-tenth of their income to the Crown. This money had previously gone to Rome.

As a result of the Reformation Parliament, Henry's dispute with the Pope had been escalated to a full-blown division between him and the Roman Catholic Church. Henry no longer recognised the Pope as head of the Church in England, and instead he saw himself in that role. The Church of England had been born, and anyone who disputed Henry's right to be its head was dismissed from office, imprisoned or executed. Two high-profile victims to suffer death were John Fisher, the Bishop of Rochester, and his former Lord Chancellor and close friend, Sir Thomas More, both of whom were executed in 1535, despite the fact that Henry had promised More he would not have to get involved in the marriage debate.

We read in the account of Edward Hall, published in 1542:

This year also on 17th June was arraigned at Westminster in the king's bench John Fisher, bishop of Rochester, for treason against the king, and he was condemned there by a jury of knights and esquires (the lord chancellor sitting as high judge …) The effect of the treason was denying the king to be Supreme Head of the Church of England, according to a statute, The Act of Supremacy, made in the last session of Parliament …

On 22nd June, Tuesday, John Fisher, bishop of Rochester, was beheaded at Tower Hill. His body was buried in Barking churchyard, next to the Tower of London, and his head was set on London Bridge.

This year also on 1st July, being Thursday, Sir Thomas More, sometime chancellor of England, was arraigned at Westminster for high treason and there condemned, and the Tuesday after, being 6th July, he was beheaded at Tower Hill and his body was buried within the chapel in the Tower of London, and his head was set on London Bridge. The effect of his death was for the same cause that the bishop of Rochester died for.

Sir Thomas More maintained a prolonged silence in the Tower of London, believing that this would save his life. A letter from More to his daughter, written the day before his execution, survives, in which he wrote: 'Farewell, my dear child, and pray for me, and I shall for you and all your friends, that we may merrily meet in heaven.' At the end, More declared: 'I die the King's good servant, but God's first.'

And so, while there had been no significant changes to the teachings, beliefs or practices of the Church, a fundamental break with the Church in Rome had been effected – usually referred to as 'the break from Rome' – which was to clear the way for yet more radical changes in the years ahead.

Exercise 2.2

1 Write a few sentences to explain the meaning of the following:

   (a) Indulgences

   (b) *Fidei Defensor*

   (c) Purgatory

2 Look at Thomas Wolsey's career as Henry VIII's chief minister. Create a table with columns labelled Finance, Justice, Foreign Policy and The Church. Make a list of Wolsey's accomplishments and failures in each column.

3 Explain how successful Thomas Wolsey was as Henry VIII's chief minister.

Exercise 2.3

Read the following sources about Henry VIII's Great Matter and answer the questions that follow.

SOURCE A: From an English summary of Julius II's Papal Dispensation of 1503, allowing Henry to marry Catherine of Aragon in 1509.

The Pope has received a petition from Prince Henry and Princess Catherine ... When the Princess was married to Prince Arthur, he died with no children. Prince Henry and Princess Catherine now desire to marry to preserve the peace between England and Spain. The Pope grants their request and allows them to marry.

SOURCE B: From a letter written by Henry to Anne Boleyn during the late 1520s.

My own sweetheart, these letters are to tell you of the great loneliness that I find here since you left, for I think it feels longer than a whole fortnight. I wish I could be (especially in the evening) in my sweetheart's arms, and I long to kiss you. Written by the one that was, is, and shall be yours.

SOURCE C: From *English Reformations* by Christopher Haigh, published in 1993.

We do not know whether Henry decided to divorce Catherine of Aragon because he had fallen for Anne, or whether he fell for Anne when he had already decided to divorce Catherine. Probably the two processes ... went together, encouraged by Anne's refusal to become a mere mistress ... Enticed by the prospects of a new wife and a son who would surely follow, Henry easily convinced himself that he was free to marry Anne.

1 What can you learn from Source A about the reasons for Henry marrying Catherine?

2 How far do Sources B and C agree on why Henry wanted to divorce Catherine of Aragon?

3 Which of Sources B and C do you think is more useful to a historian? Explain your answer.

4 Using all the sources and your own knowledge, how far do you agree with the view that politics was more important than love in the King's Great Matter?

Dissolution of the Monasteries, 1536–40

One result of Henry's break from Rome which caused him concern was the effect it might have on other powers in Europe, most obviously the Kings of Spain and France. At the time of his excommunication of Henry, the Pope had actively encouraged both Francis I of France and Charles V of Spain, the Holy Roman Emperor, to declare war on Henry as an enemy of the Church. War would require funds, and although, as a result of the Act for First Fruits and Tenths of 1534, Henry now had access to Church revenues which had previously been channelled back to the Pope in Rome, he knew that this would not be enough.

···PROCEDE TO THE DISSOLUTION AND THE DEFACING···1558

■ An illustration depicting the Dissolution of the Monasteries

In 1535, Henry gave Cromwell the title Vicegerent, or Vicar General, and this allowed him to interfere in Church affairs. Cromwell realised that the Church in England was immensely wealthy, and that one area of its wealth which might easily be diverted to the Crown was that of the monasteries. In the 1520s, as we saw above, Cromwell had assisted Wolsey in closing down some of the most obviously corrupt monasteries, and he now saw an opportunity to extend this to the other monasteries.

Catholics believed that monasteries were holy places housing monks who withdrew from the world and prayed to God on behalf of people, allowing them to gain speedy escape from Purgatory. To some Protestants, on the other hand, although the monasteries were highly regarded as centres of learning, they were also seen as examples of the worst sort of excess within the Church, with their huge wealth either enabling the monks themselves to live lives of drunken debauchery, or else providing a vast source of income for the Pope in Rome. Either way, they felt that radical reform of the monasteries was called for.

In England at this time, there were 502 abbeys, 136 nunneries and 187 friaries, all of which now came under Henry's control as head of the English Church. Cromwell sent out two groups of commissioners to report on these religious houses. One group recorded the wealth and income of the monasteries (forming a survey called the *Valor Ecclesiasticus*). The other investigated allegations of corruption or clerical abuses. The reports made mixed comments about the monasteries, but it is likely that Cromwell made clear to the commissioners that stories of corruption were what he wanted to hear.

One of the commissioners wrote to Cromwell in 1535:

> *I went to Godstow where I found all things in good order, both in the monastery and the convent, except that one sister, 13 or 14 years ago, when in another house, had broken her chastity. For her correction and punishment, the Bishop of Lincoln sent her to Godstow, where she has now lived in virtue ever since. From there I went to Eynsham where I found a raw sort of religious persons. All kind of sin had been committed by them, for which offences they have now been punished by the local bishop. As far as I can tell, the abbot is chaste of living and right well supervises the repairs of his house. He is negligent in the overseeing of the brethren but claims that this is because of his daily illness, which infirmity did appear, by his face, to be true.*

In 1536, Cromwell drew up the results of his commission and presented a bill for the dissolution of the smaller monasteries to Parliament. This was an excuse to test the opposition to the bill before continuing with the full process of dissolution. The bill roundly attacked the religious establishments:

> *Manifest sin, vicious, carnal and abominable living is daily used and committed amongst the little and small abbeys, priories and other such religious houses of monks, canons and nuns, where the congregation of such religious persons is under the number of twelve persons. The governors of such houses consume and waste the ornaments of their churches and their goods and chattels to the high displeasure of Almighty God, slander of good religion and to the great infamy of the King's Highness and the realm, if redress should not be had. There can be no reformation unless such small houses are utterly suppressed ...*

As soon as the bill had gone through Parliament, Cromwell began the dissolution. Although only empowered to close down the smaller monasteries, in practice little distinction was made between these and the larger ones, and when a further act was passed in 1539 permitting the dissolution of the larger monasteries, it was widely seen as simply legalising what was already happening.

Cromwell was helped in his task by the greed of local landowners. For, although he had rightly feared that the process of dissolution might meet with resistance, selling off the lands and buildings to local landowners proved immensely popular. As for the monks and nuns – for it should be remembered that nunneries were affected no less than monasteries – they were powerless to resist.

The Pilgrimage of Grace, 1536

Opposition to the closure of the monasteries, when it came, was forceful and led to a collection of risings against the King, mainly in the north, which became known as the Pilgrimage of Grace. When Cromwell's commissioners arrived in Lincolnshire to close down the monasteries in that county, they encountered a violent protest which led to around 10 000 men attacking Lincoln and occupying the cathedral. A force led by the Duke of Suffolk came to face the rebels, who rapidly dispersed.

News of the Lincoln rising travelled north to Yorkshire, however, and here opposition was more threatening. Led by the lawyer Robert Aske and Lord Darcy, a large body of rebels numbering as many as 30 000 gathered together and marched on York. It is difficult from their published demands to be sure what these men were actually complaining about, and how far their demands were strictly religious. They demanded an end to heresy, that heretical bishops, chiefly Cranmer, should be deposed and that those responsible for the Dissolution of the Monasteries should be punished. In the petition drawn up by Aske in December 1536, they demanded that Mary be declared legitimate and that certain acts of the Reformation Parliament, such as the Treason Act, be repealed. But they also wished enclosure to be halted, parliamentary elections to be reformed and the abuses of corrupt officials to be ended.

Aske claimed that he was leading not a rebellion, but rather a pilgrimage designed to free Henry from the advice of evil heretics such as Cromwell. Those who followed him swore an oath that made this clear:

Ye shall not enter into this Pilgrimage of Grace for the Commonwealth, but only for the love that ye do bear unto Almighty God his faith, and the Holy Church ... to the preservation of the King's person and his issue, to purifying of the nobility, and to expulse all villein blood and evil councillors against the Commonwealth from his Grace and his Privy Council ...

The rebels marched south, as the chronicler Edward Hall, who clearly disapproved of them, describes:

They had certain banners in the field whereon was painted Christ hanging on the cross on one side, and a chalice with a painted cake in it on the other side, with various other banners of similar hypocrisy and feigned sanctity. The

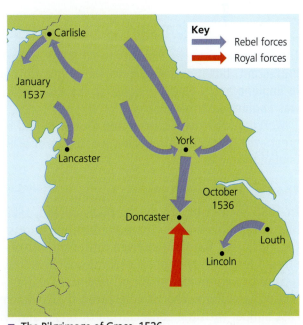

Key
↦ Rebel forces
↦ Royal forces

Carlisle
January 1537
Lancaster
York
Doncaster
October 1536
Louth
Lincoln

■ The Pilgrimage of Grace, 1536

soldiers also had a certain badge embroidered upon the sleeves of their coats which was a representation of the five wounds of Christ, and in the midst thereof was written the name of Our Lord, and thus the rebellious garrison of Satan set forth and decked themselves with his false and counterfeited signs of holiness, only to delude and deceive the simple and ignorant people.

Their progress caused Henry considerable alarm. Never before had he faced opposition to his plans like this, and the forces available to him to suppress the rebels were inadequate. He sent the Duke of Norfolk to head them off, with clear instructions not to allow them to make further progress towards London.

Norfolk met the rebels at Doncaster and played for time. He knew that many of Aske's men would be unwilling to leave their homes for long, and so after much deliberating with Aske and the other leaders, he agreed to pardon all those who had taken part in the pilgrimage and to summon a Parliament to hear their complaints. The rebels dispersed, but no such Parliament was ever called and instead Aske was arrested and executed in York, along with over 170 of the ringleaders.

The Pilgrimage of Grace had caused Henry a nasty shock, but it changed nothing. The monasteries, which Aske had described at his trial as 'one of the great beauties of this realm', were gone for good. Their libraries were plundered and the poor lost a great source of help in times of trouble. But Henry had gained a huge increase in his annual revenues as a result, perhaps as much as double what he had enjoyed before, and that was all that mattered to him.

Protestantism and Catholicism

The Dissolution of the Monasteries did not make England more Protestant, but it certainly gave Henry greater control of the Church in England and a valuable boost to his finances. So how Protestant was England at this time?

Working together, Cranmer and Cromwell had been exploiting the break with Rome to introduce a limited form of Protestantism into England.

The Ten Articles of 1536

In 1536 the **Act of Ten Articles** was passed, taking the Protestant line of recognising only three sacraments: baptism, penance and the Eucharist. **Baptism** allowed full entry into the Church; **penance** offered forgiveness of one's sins for one who truly repented, in return for performing an act of penance, such as saying prayers or fasting; and the Eucharist celebrated the commemoration of Christ's Last Supper with the consecration of bread and wine. The four other

Catholic sacraments, confirmation, ordination, marriage and the last rites, continued to be practised but were no longer seen as being holy sacraments. A great many holy days (from which we get the word holiday) were abolished, a Bible in English was made available, and priests were given permission to marry.

Perhaps buoyed by the failure of the Pilgrimage of Grace, Cromwell then decided to go even further in his moves towards making England a more Protestant land. He clamped down on the display of relics, prohibited pilgrimages, and – most dramatically – ordered the destruction of the tomb of Thomas Becket at Canterbury and the shrine of the Virgin Mary at Walsingham.

But if Cromwell thought this would be popular with Henry, he was wrong. Henry had flirted, briefly, with Protestant ideas but was really only interested in them to the extent that they would benefit him, politically or financially. Now that he was head of the Church of England, and was enjoying the wealth of the monasteries, Henry was more than happy to leave religious practices alone. In essence, Henry VIII was an 'English Catholic' – a Catholic in belief, but one who didn't obey the Pope.

The Six Articles of 1539

As Henry grew impatient with Cromwell's religious changes, so he determined to reverse much of what Cromwell had introduced. The Six Articles of 1539 saw a return to Catholic beliefs, and a renewed commitment to some of the doctrines that Protestants so bitterly opposed. These included:

- transubstantiation (the belief that the bread and wine used during the Eucharist changed into the substance of the body and blood of Christ when consecrated)
- clerical celibacy (preventing priests from getting married)
- the importance of confession (confessing one's sins to a priest in private)
- the taking at communion of the bread only (Protestants thought that the people should take both bread and wine; Catholics thought that only the priest need take both bread and wine).

Penalties were imposed on all who refused to accept the provisions of the Six Articles, which angry Protestants referred to as 'the whip with six strings'. In 1543 Henry went even further in his rejection of Protestant ideas with the publication of the *King's Book*, which prevented 'women or artificers, apprentices, journeymen, serving men of the degrees of yeomen or under, husbandmen and labourers' from reading the newly translated English Bible.

Clearly, Henry VIII was far from convinced by the Protestant ideas that were causing such a stir across Europe.

There is a well-known ditty that records the various fates of Henry's wives:

Divorced, beheaded, died;

Divorced, beheaded, survived.

We have already seen how the first one, Catherine of Aragon, came to be discarded. We will now look at how the others fared.

Henry VIII, as we learnt on page 9, had been from his youth extremely interested in religious matters and when his marriage to Anne Boleyn failed to produce the longed-for son, he began to question whether he was being punished by God. The love that had brought the two together faded, and Henry looked around for an escape from a marriage that had not brought him the thing he most needed: a son. This became particularly pressing when Henry fell in love once more, this time with the young and beautiful Jane Seymour.

The fall of Anne Boleyn

Once again, Henry turned to Cromwell to solve his problem, and Cromwell came up with a charge of adultery and treason. He produced evidence that Anne had committed adultery on several occasions, not least with her own brother, Lord Rochford, and that she was plotting to murder Henry. A rumour was also spread that Anne – who had never been popular with the English people – was a witch, and had bewitched Henry. Whether there was any truth in the charges or not, Anne and her brother were executed. Even one of Anne's greatest critics, the Spanish ambassador Eustace Chapuys, was aware that the case against Anne – whom he refers to as 'the whore' – was unconvincing:

■ Anne Boleyn; a sixteenth-century portrait

Although everybody rejoices at the execution of the whore there are some who murmur at the mode of procedure against her and the others, and people speak variously of the king; and it will not pacify the world when it is known what has passed and is passing between him and Jane Seymour.

As for Anne herself, she was gracious towards Henry at the end, but determined to defend her honour, stating at her trial:

I do not say that I have always borne the king the humility which I owed him, considering his kindness and the great honour he showed me; I admit too that often I have taken it into my head to be jealous of him … But may God be my witness if I have done him any other wrong.

And at her execution, according to the account in John Stow's *Annals of England*, published in 1601, she maintained her great dignity:

All these being on a scaffold made there for the execution, the said Queen Anne said as followeth: 'Masters, I here humbly submit me to the law, as the law hath judged me, and as for mine offences, God knoweth them, I remit them to God, beseeching him to have mercy on my soul; and I beseech Jesu save my Sovereign and master the King, the most goodliest, and gentlest Prince that is, and long to reign over you'; which words she spake with a smiling countenance: which done, she kneeled down on both her knees, and said, 'To Jesu Christ I commend my soul' and with that word suddenly the hangman of Calais smote off her head at one stroke with a sword: her body with the head was buried in the choir of the Chapel in the Tower.

Jane Seymour

With Anne out of the way, Cranmer annulled the marriage, making Princess Elizabeth illegitimate. Henry was once again free to marry, and a few days after Anne's execution in May 1536, he married Jane Seymour. In October 1537, Jane gave birth to the son Henry had so longed for but there were complications with the birth and, twelve days later, Jane died. The child was christened Edward. Jane was buried in St George's Chapel, Windsor, and when Henry himself died ten years later, he was buried next to her.

Anne of Cleves

Henry's fourth marriage, to Anne of Cleves, took place in 1540 and lasted only six months. At this time, Cromwell was concerned about the possibility of an invasion by the forces of France and Charles V, the Holy Roman Emperor and King of Spain. He thought that an alliance with the Duke of Cleves, an enemy of France and Spain, would be useful, and so suggested that Henry should marry the Duke's sister, Anne.

Henry knew nothing about Anne, and sent the painter Hans Holbein to paint a portrait of her, so that he could make a decision as to whether to marry her or not. On the strength of this painting, Henry decided to marry her.

■ Anne of Cleves; from a painting by Hans Holbein the Younger, 1539

However, when Anne came over for the wedding, Henry found that Holbein had greatly exaggerated the lady's good looks. He found that she was far from attractive, and is said to have called her the 'Flanders mare'. 'I am ashamed that men have so praised her as they have done, and I like her not,' he said. On his wedding day he is reported to have said to Cromwell:

My Lord, if it were not to satisfy the world, and my Realm, I would not do that I must do this day for none earthly thing.

Henry was furious with Cromwell for his part in the marriage arrangements, and his enemies seized their opportunity to get rid of him. Notable among his enemies was the Duke of Norfolk, whose niece, Catherine Howard, had at this time come to Henry's attention. Knowing that Henry was angry with Cromwell over the marriage, and was disillusioned with Cromwell's efforts to introduce increasingly Protestant changes, Norfolk persuaded the King that Cromwell was guilty of heresy. Henry, who was growing more vicious the older he became, had Cromwell arrested and in July 1540 he was executed at the Tower of London. His last words from the scaffold proclaimed his innocence: 'Many have slandered me, and reported that I have been a bearer of evil opinions; which is untrue.'

Catherine Howard

Henry quickly had his disastrous marriage to Anne annulled and then married Catherine Howard. Henry was infatuated with Catherine and called her his 'Rose without a thorn'. However, Catherine was soon accused of adultery and, unlike her cousin Anne Boleyn, the charges laid against Catherine appear to have been true. Henry was unwilling at first to believe the evidence against his pretty young wife, but reluctantly came to accept it. Catherine and her lovers were executed in 1542.

Catherine Parr

Henry's last wife was Catherine Parr, whom he married in 1543. Catherine was a dutiful wife who helped Henry become reconciled with his two daughters. Realising that he only had one heir, and a sickly one at that, Henry was persuaded to declare that his daughters, who had earlier been declared illegitimate, should be able to inherit the throne. On 30 December 1546 he made his will, bequeathing his throne to his son Edward, then to any children he might have with Catherine Parr, then to Mary, then to Elizabeth, and finally to the daughters of his sister Mary, the French Queen. As things turned out, this was to be extremely significant, for both Mary and Elizabeth went on to become queen.

How accurate is the rhyme that begins 'Divorced, beheaded, died ...'? Did Henry VIII 'divorce' his first and fourth wives in the way we understand the term?

⃝ The end of Henry's reign

Henry VIII died in London on 28 January 1547. He had been a strong king, ruthless when necessary and cruel at times. He will always be remembered for having had six wives, for his break with Rome, and for his part in the Dissolution of the Monasteries. But actually, as we have seen, he died very much a Catholic, critical of the religious beliefs of Cromwell and others, and still committed to the religion in which he himself had been brought up, albeit without a Pope to interfere.

Perhaps his most lasting contribution to English history stems from his choice of tutors for his son Edward, who were sympathetic to Protestant teachings. By educating the heir to the throne in the new Protestant tradition, he was, perhaps unwittingly, allowing a full-scale rejection of Catholicism in the years to come.

Exercise 2.4

1 Write a sentence or two to explain the meaning of the following:

(a) Baptism

(b) Penance

(c) The Eucharist

(d) The Six Articles

(e) The *King's Book*

2 Explain the reasons Henry VIII and Cromwell had for dissolving the monasteries.

3 Explain the consequences of the Dissolution of the Monasteries.

Exercise 2.5

1 List the six wives of Henry VIII. Give:

(a) the reasons for the marriage

(b) the children the marriage produced, if any

(c) the fate of the wife.

2 Choose one of the wives and write a series of entries in her diary.

Exercise 2.6

How successful were Henry VIII's changes to the Church in England?

■ The Presence Chamber, Hampton Court; from *The Mansions of England in the Olden Time* by Joseph Nash, 1520s

Edward VI and Mary I

Edward VI, 1547–53

Edward VI became king in 1547 at the ripe old age of nine, in succession to his father Henry VIII. His reign was to last just six years, but it witnessed great religious and political change which then ushered in a period of even greater religious turmoil as his sister, 'Bloody Mary', undid the changes of his reign.

■ Edward VI; from a portrait produced in the sixteenth century

Edward had been born in 1537, the long-awaited son of Henry VIII and his third wife, Jane Seymour. He was serious and studious, well versed in Latin, Greek and French, and often described as 'old beyond his years'. His father placed his education in the hands of tutors who were sympathetic to the Protestant ideas spreading across from Europe, ideas which had been warmly embraced by Henry's close advisors such as Thomas Cromwell, but which he himself had rejected.

On his accession, Edward was too young to rule himself, and so a Regency Council was appointed to exercise power on his behalf. This council was initially controlled by Edward's uncle, Edward Seymour, the Duke of Somerset, but later came under the control of John Dudley, Earl of Warwick, soon to be Duke of Northumberland, who ousted Somerset and took the role of Lord President of the Council in 1549.

Cranmer and the Protestant surge

Somerset and Northumberland were both keen Protestants who favoured the religious changes that Cromwell had been embracing. No sooner was Henry VIII dead than Somerset, who had been appointed by Henry as Protector for the young Edward, set about dismantling Catholicism. Many of the Catholic rituals and ceremonies that had been part of English life for centuries were banned. These included such colourful occasions as the Corpus Christi processions, when consecrated bread, which Catholics believed had been transformed into the body of Christ, was carried through the streets in a special shrine. The procession was accompanied by great celebrations, as was the St George's Day ceremony, when statues of St George and the dragon were carried through the streets, watched by people dressed in costumes and enjoying the drama and colour of the occasion. Gone, too, were the Easter rituals of 'creeping to the cross' on Good Friday, and those of the Easter sepulchre. There were many other such customs, part of the very fabric of English life, which were now, quite suddenly, banned.

Somerset was also quick to set up an enquiry into the state of the Church in England. Commissioners were sent out into every parish and their findings led to the following, hastily drawn up measures:

- The Chantries Act in 1547 abolished **chantries**. These were chapels to which people left money on the understanding that masses would be said there after their death. People believed that the saying of masses after death would speed up the process of freeing their souls from Purgatory. The Chantries Act abolished the chantries, and caused all their money and property to be handed over to the Crown.
- The Act of Uniformity in 1549 imposed a single, standard form of worship across England, which everyone was obliged to follow. For the first time, English, not Latin, was to be used as the language of worship, and both bread and wine were to be given during communion. A new Prayer Book was introduced, compiled by Archbishop Cranmer. Notable in the 1549 Prayer Book was the fact that Cranmer was rather vague on the crucial matter of transubstantiation. He neither endorsed it nor wholly rejected it, and some fervent Protestants were dissatisfied as a result.

Protestantism and John Calvin

Cranmer had been introducing Protestant ideas into the English Church which were essentially Lutheran. But the ideas of Martin Luther had been taken further by a French Protestant called John Calvin. Calvin was even more critical of the Catholic Church than Luther had been, and encouraged Protestants to set up new churches. Calvin believed in **predestination**, the idea that God decides who will go to Heaven and who will go to Hell, before each person is born. Those chosen for Heaven, 'the elect', can be recognised by their good behaviour; those chosen for Hell, 'the reprobate', can be recognised by their bad behaviour. Either way, no one needs the intervention of priests or saints, and no one needs to buy indulgences.

The strict moral code of behaviour that Calvin encouraged included wearing simple clothes, having short hair, avoiding music and games, closing down theatres, abandoning popular holiday activities such as maypole dancing, removing all the ornaments and colourful decoration from churches and much more besides. These ideas were developed further by people called the **Puritans** (see Chapter 4) and would certainly not have been tolerated by Henry VIII. And yet, his son was to rule over a country that saw Calvinist ideas develop extremely rapidly.

1549: A year of rebellions

Edward faced two significant rebellions during his reign, both in 1549. The first of these seems to have been a direct response to the religious changes introduced in the first two years of the reign. The second was more to do with economic hardships.

The Western Rebellion (April 1549)	Kett's Rebellion (July 1549)
Causes: • People in Cornwall and Devon did not like the imposition of Edward's religious changes. • They objected in particular to the Chantries Act and the new Prayer Book, especially because it was in English. • Concern about new taxes. Demands: • Re-instatement of the Six Articles. • Return to old Catholic forms of worship. • A delay in further religious changes. Events: • Opponents marched on the city of Exeter and besieged it. • Government had no control over the area for some two months. • Protector Somerset sent Lord Russell to remove the rebels. • Several small battles resulted and the rebels were scattered. 2500 people were killed.	Causes: • Opposition to enclosure in East Anglia. • High land rents. • Loss of common fishing rights in rivers and the sea. Events: • A force was gathered, led by Robert Kett. The city of Norwich was captured by the rebels. • Government troops were pushed back. • Fresh troops led by the Earl of Warwick defeated the rebels at the Battle of Mousehold Heath. About 3000 of Kett's 16 000 men were killed in the battle. • Kett was captured and executed for treason on 7 December 1549.

The Prayer Book of 1552 and the Forty-Two Articles

Following the defeat of the Western Rebellion of 1549, and ignoring the demands of the rebels for a return to the religion of Henry VIII's later years, Cranmer made further religious changes and introduced a revised Prayer Book in 1552, known as the *Book of Common Prayer*, which was more Protestant than the first (for example, it removed the concept of transubstantiation), and was very close to the views of Calvin.

In 1553, he then published his Forty-Two Articles, written 'for the avoiding of controversy in opinions' and which showed clearly how much Protestant ideas now dominated the teachings of the Church of England. It was made compulsory for all clergy, schoolmasters and students at the universities to subscribe to these articles.

The end of the reign

As a teenager, Edward's health declined and when in the spring of 1552 he caught first measles and then smallpox, there were fears for his life. He recovered, but then succumbed to tuberculosis and died in 1553.

The *Book of Common Prayer* is still used, in a modified form, today. It is responsible for many phrases that have found their way into everyday English. Can you find out what some of them are?

Exercise 3.1

Write a few sentences on each of the following:

1 The Dukes of Somerset and Northumberland

2 John Calvin

3 The Act of Uniformity of 1549

4 The Prayer Books of 1549 and 1552

Exercise 3.2

SOURCE A: The allegorical painting of Edward VI below represents the triumph of Protestantism over the Catholic Church. The painting, produced around 1570, shows: in his bed, the dying Henry VIII; Edward VI sitting on the throne; to his left, Protector Somerset and the Privy Council; the Pope, with his head bent, in the foreground; outside, reformers smashing statues of the saints and the Virgin Mary.

■ Edward VI; a painting produced around 1570 by an anonymous artist

SOURCE B: An extract from Edward VI's journal for the year 1551, recording a visit paid to him by his Catholic sister, Mary.

The lady Mary, my sister, came to me to Westminster, where after greetings she was called with my council into a chamber where it was declared how long I had suffered her mass, in hope of her reconciliation; and how now, there being no hope as I saw by her letters, unless I saw some speedy amendment, I could not bear it. She answered that her soul was God's and her faith she would not change, nor hide her opinion with dissembled doings.

SOURCE C: An extract from a 1551 letter to Edward VI from John Calvin, warning the King against Catholic practices.

We must always observe the rule that there must be sobriety and moderation in ceremonies, so that the light of the gospel be not obscured ... For God does not allow any one to sport with his name, mingling frivolities with his holy and sacred works. Now there are many abuses which cannot be endured; for instance, prayer for the dead, placing before God in our prayers the intercession of saints, and adding their names to his in taking an oath. I doubt not, sire, that you have been informed of these things: I implore you in the name of God to persevere, so that everything may be restored to its proper integrity ... God wishes to commend highly those faithful princes who have restored and re-established the purity of his service ...

1 Look at Source A. What do you think the picture is trying to show?

2 Read Source B. How does it add to the picture of religious life under Edward given in Source A?

3 Read Source C. What does it tell you about the religious teaching that Edward received from his advisors?

4 Using all the sources and your own knowledge, how far had England become Protestant at the end of Edward VI's reign?

Exercise 3.3

1 Look at the extract below, taken from the demands of the rebels in Devon and Cornwall. Write a few sentences to explain what you can learn from this about the reasons for the Western Rebellion in 1549.

First we will have the general council and holy decrees of our forefathers observed, kept and performed, and who so ever shall gainsay them, we hold as heretics.

2 Look at the table on page 34 setting out the details of the Western Rebellion and Kett's Rebellion. What similarities and differences are there between the two rebellions of 1549?

Lady Jane Grey: the nine-day queen

The death of Edward VI without an heir led to a period of political and religious upheaval, the likes of which England had never seen before. England, as we have seen, was by 1553 officially a Protestant country, with an established Church which now ran counter to the teachings of the Roman Catholic Church on a wide range of matters. The next in line to the throne, however, in the absence of a suitable male heir, was Mary, the eldest daughter of Henry VIII and a fanatical Roman Catholic.

Mary was the daughter of Henry VIII and Catherine of Aragon. As a committed Roman Catholic, she had continued to practise her religion under Edward, as we can see in Source B on page 36. Edward's advisors, notably Northumberland, were horrified at the prospect of having a Roman Catholic monarch, and did what they could to avoid it. As Edward lay on his deathbed, and with the assistance of Cranmer, the Archbishop of Canterbury, Northumberland persuaded the dying King to name as his successor, not his Catholic sister Mary or his Protestant sister Elizabeth, on the grounds that they were both illegitimate, but the Protestant Lady Jane Grey. Jane was the granddaughter of Henry VIII's sister Mary and the scheming Northumberland, while plotting to ensure that Jane was named as Edward's heir, had arranged for her to be married to his son, Guildford Dudley.

However, despite the fact that she was Protestant, and Mary was Catholic, Lady Jane Grey received little support for her claim, and when Mary rode into London in August 1553, she was greeted as the rightful queen. The fifteen-year-old Jane was arrested and locked up in the Tower of London, together with her father and husband. Her nine-day reign was at an end.

Most chronologies do not include Lady Jane Grey as queen between Edward VI and Mary I. Why do you think this is? Can you find any other examples of English 'monarchs' who are not generally regarded as such?

Mary I, 1553–58

When Mary entered London in 1553 with Elizabeth at her side, to be greeted by cheering crowds, she believed that the Protestant experiments of her father, and more seriously her brother, were over. She believed that her people, like her, resented the changes that had been made to the religious life of the country, and that they, like her, were keen to restore Roman Catholicism in all its papal glory. She was wrong.

Mary had not had a happy childhood. Her father had divorced her Spanish mother, Catherine of Aragon, when she was still a

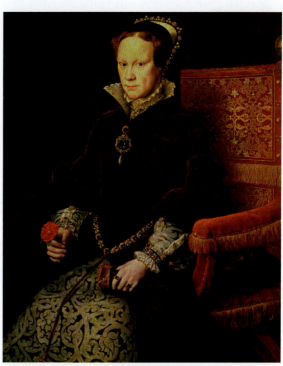

■ Mary I; a portrait produced in 1554 by Sir Anthonis Mor van Dashorst (Antonio Moro)

teenager, and then very publicly declared by Act of Parliament that she, Mary, was illegitimate. Mary was deeply affected by this, and she never forgot the way her father had manipulated religion to bring about the annulment of his marriage. She had then been separated from her mother, and prevented from seeing her, even when her mother lay dying. And after her father's death, she had been put under great pressure by her brother's advisors to give up her religion and embrace the new Protestant teachings. She refused, and continued to worship as a Catholic.

When Mary came to the throne in 1553, she was 37 years old. She saw it as her mission to restore Catholicism to England and, seeing the need to secure an heir, turned to Spain to provide her with a husband. Her cousin Philip – soon to become Philip II of Spain – seemed the obvious choice, and in 1554 she invited him to England.

Wyatt's Rebellion, 1554

Philip was one of the most powerful men in Europe, and in some ways the marriage might have been seen as a shrewd move to link the fortunes of England to those of Spain. But Mary had misjudged the strength of feeling in the country towards foreigners. A son born to Mary and Philip would have been heir to the thrones of both countries; he would, most certainly, have been Catholic, but more importantly, he would have been Spanish, and England would have been ruled as a Spanish province. This was to be avoided at all costs. So when the large Spanish delegation arrived in London, rebellion broke out.

As we read in John Foxe's *Book of Martyrs*, a strongly anti-Catholic tract published in 1563:

The premature death of that celebrated young monarch, Edward VI, occasioned the most extraordinary and wonderful occurrences, which had ever existed from the times of our blessed Lord and Saviour's incarnation in human shape. This melancholy event became speedily a subject of general regret. The succession to the English throne was soon made a matter of contention; and the scenes which ensued were a demonstration of the serious affliction in which the kingdom was involved.

The rebellion against Mary that broke out in 1554 was led by Sir Thomas Wyatt. Wyatt plotted to overthrow

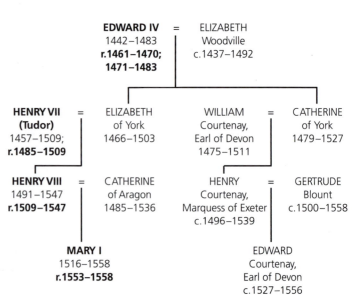

■ Family tree showing the connection of Edward Courtenay to the House of Tudor

Mary and replace her with Edward Courtenay, the great-grandson of Edward IV (see family tree, page 38). The idea was that Edward would then marry Mary's sister Elizabeth, thus keeping the Crown in the Tudor family, and an English Protestant dynasty would be assured. Around 3000 rebels marched to London, overcame the small force of royal soldiers, and paraded through the city. However, the citizens remained loyal to Mary, who boldly explained to them that her proposed marriage was in the public interest, and that she herself was unafraid of the rebels. Addressing some of the leading citizens at London's Guildhall in January she said:

> *... And on the word of a Queen, I promise you, that if it shall not appear to all the nobility and commons that this marriage shall be for the high benefit and commodity of the realm, then I will abstain from marriage while I live. And now good subjects, pluck up your hearts, and like true men, stand fast against these rebels; and fear them not, for, I assure you, I fear them nothing at all.*

The rebellion thus failed and 120 of the rebels were hanged. Wyatt himself was brutally executed and his head stuck on a spike as a warning to others. As for the marriage to Philip, that went ahead as planned.

Fired with determination to defend her throne from all who might threaten her, Mary then decided that Lady Jane Grey should also be removed as a threat, lest she become the focus for future risings. Jane and her husband Guildford Dudley were executed on 12 February 1554, followed by Jane's father, the Duke of Suffolk, eleven days later. Although Elizabeth claimed not to have co-operated with the rebels in any way, she was nonetheless locked up in the Tower before being sent to the Palace at Woodstock where she lived effectively as a prisoner. As for Cranmer, who had signed the document handing the throne over to Lady Jane Grey, he was arrested on the grounds of treason and held in the Tower.

■ The execution of Lady Jane Grey; from an 1833 painting by Paul Delaroche

Catholic resurgence

Buoyed by this success, Mary then set about overturning the Reformation and restoring Roman Catholicism to England. She appointed a new Archbishop of Canterbury, her second cousin Reginald Pole, who, as a prominent Yorkist and devout Roman Catholic, had spent the previous two reigns in exile in Italy. He was now given the task of helping Mary to make England Roman Catholic once more.

Under pressure from Mary and Pole, the House of Commons agreed to remove all religious laws passed since 1529, including the 1534 Act of Supremacy, which meant the Pope was reinstated as head of the English Church. Mary could not afford to reverse the Dissolution of the Monasteries, but church services were once again to be held in Latin, the Protestant Prayer Book was outlawed, and priests were once more forbidden from marrying. Those who had already married were to leave their families and move to a new parish. Priestly **vestments**, church decoration, saints' days, statues and altar screens, all the trappings of Catholicism were restored. Parliament also reinstated the law which stated that the penalty for heresy was burning at the stake. Mary, a fanatical Catholic, thought it her duty to save heretics – in other words those who had embraced Protestantism – and this meant burning their evil bodies to allow their souls to find mercy at God's hands.

However, it was one thing to get rid of Edward VI's laws; it was quite another to persuade everyone that a full restoration of Roman Catholicism was a good idea. As might be expected, the gentry and aristocracy did not want to return lands which they had acquired since the Dissolution of the Monasteries, even if they were happy to become Catholic again. Protestant pamphlets and propaganda from Europe (where many Protestants had fled into exile) seemed more effective in promoting Protestantism than the efforts of Mary and Pole were in promoting Catholicism. In the south and east, where Protestantism was strongest, Mary and Pole's policies were often bitterly resisted.

Mary now used two methods to achieve her ends: education and persecution. Better training and supervision of parish priests were introduced, with bishops instructed to set up local training schools and make regular visits to observe the work of the priests in their area.

But then came persecution, and the reign of terror. Protestants who refused to renounce the new religion were arrested and, in February 1555, the burnings began. 'Turn or burn' was the motto of the time. Priests such as John Rogers, Vicar of St Sepulchre's, and Lawrence Saunders, Vicar in the parish of Bread Street, were among the first to be burnt. Bishops such as John Hooper, Nicholas Ridley and Hugh Latimer soon followed. Simple members of the public, like the 68-year-old crippled painter Hugh Laverick, the widow Catharine Hut of Bocking, and the spinster Elizabeth Thackwel of Great Burstead, all joined the long list of martyrs recorded in such gory detail by Foxe in his *Book of Martyrs*. To remain a Protestant, openly, was to risk death.

The death of Cranmer, 1556

But perhaps the most dramatic of all the burnings was that of Thomas Cranmer who, as Archbishop of Canterbury under Henry VIII and Edward VI, had been so instrumental in the religious changes that Mary was so keen to reverse.

Cranmer, probably against his will, had signed the document drawn up while Edward VI lay on his deathbed, granting the throne to Lady Jane Grey. When Mary took the throne, Cranmer was thus seen by her as a traitor. Possibly out of revenge for the part that he had played in the divorce of her parents, rather than any real concern about his loyalty to the Crown, Cranmer was accused of treason and imprisoned in the Tower of London.

Cranmer was then taken to Oxford to defend himself against the charge of heresy. Here he was persuaded by his replacement as Archbishop of Canterbury, the Catholic Reginald Pole, to recant his Protestant views.

Terrified and fearful for his life, he tried to save himself by signing a series of documents which, according to the account of Foxe, concluded:

> *Finally, in all things I profess, that I do not otherwise believe than the Catholic Church and the Church of Rome holdeth and teacheth. I am sorry that I ever held or thought otherwise. And I beseech Almighty God, that of His mercy He will vouchsafe to forgive me whatsoever I have offended against God or His Church.*

However, this did not satisfy Pole and Cranmer was instructed to preach a sermon on the following day in the University Church of St Mary's, declaring publicly how he had embraced Catholicism once more. Cranmer was led to the church, dressed, Foxe tells us, in 'torn, dirty garb', and found the church full, with 'a low mean stage, erected opposite to the pulpit', the traces of which may still be seen today, cut into the pillars in the church.

But Cranmer had had a change of heart. He deeply regretted his cowardice in seeking to save himself, and, breaking from the agreed script, denounced his own faults, disowned the statements that he had recently signed, and committed himself to God's care. And, recognising that he would now surely face death by burning, he concluded:

> *And forasmuch as my hand hath offended, writing contrary to my heart, therefore my hand shall first be punished; for when I come to the fire it shall first be burned.*

The events that followed are dramatically told in Foxe's *Book of Martyrs*. John Foxe, a Protestant clergyman, did not actually witness the events at first hand, and the book's specific purpose was to glorify the Protestant martyrs and vilify the Catholics, so this account must be taken with caution:

> *Upon the conclusion of this unexpected declaration, amazement and indignation were conspicuous in every part of the church. The*

Catholics were completely foiled, their object being frustrated, Cranmer, like Samson, having completed a greater ruin upon his enemies in the hour of death, than he did in his life.

Cranmer would have proceeded in the exposure of the popish doctrines, but the murmurs of the idolaters drowned his voice, and the preacher gave an order to 'lead the heretic away!' The savage command was directly obeyed, and the lamb about to suffer was torn from his stand to the place of slaughter, insulted all the way by the revilings and taunts of the pestilent monks and friars.

With thoughts intent upon a far higher object than the empty threats of man, he reached the spot dyed with the blood of Ridley and Latimer. There he knelt for a short time in earnest devotion, and then arose, that he might undress and prepare for the fire. A chain was provided to bind him to the stake, and after it had tightly encircled him, fire was put to the fuel, and the flames began soon to ascend.

Then it was, that stretching out his right hand, he held it unshrinkingly in the fire until it was burnt to a cinder, frequently exclaiming, 'This unworthy right hand'.

■ Cranmer burnt as a heretic in 1556; from Foxe's *Book of Martyrs*, 1563

The persecution and burnings became more and more frequent as Mary's reign progressed. Altogether, an estimated 284 people were burnt during her reign, including five bishops, twenty-one ministers, eight gentlemen, eighty-four workers, one hundred farmers, twenty-six wives, twenty widows, nine girls, two boys and two infants. Mary regarded the executions as necessary to cleanse England of the Protestant Reformation. However, by executing people so publicly she turned many into heroes or martyrs. In particular, the high-profile burnings of Cranmer, Latimer, Hooper and Ridley backfired as more and more ordinary Protestants seemed prepared to make a stand on their faith. Instead of frightening people back to Catholicism, Mary may in fact have reinforced their Protestant beliefs.

> The place where these Protestant martyrs were burnt at the stake can be seen today, outside Balliol College in Oxford. Pay a visit if you can. How is the spot marked?

The end of Mary's reign

Mary was not a well person in the final years of her reign. Her marriage to Philip of Spain had been unpopular and had not brought her the heir that she had hoped for, despite at least two phantom pregnancies. She died in November 1558 and was buried in Westminster Abbey, where she now shares a tomb with her sister Elizabeth I. The Latin inscription on their tomb reads: 'Partners both in Throne and grave, here rest we two sisters, Elizabeth and Mary, in the hope of one resurrection.' Perhaps this can be seen as confirmation that, despite the bitter conflict between Catholics and Protestants during these years, they all looked for salvation to the same God.

Exercise 3.4

1 Read the following extract from a letter from Simon Renard, Spanish Ambassador in London, to Philip II of Spain in 1555.

The people of London are murmuring about the cruel enforcement of the recent acts of Parliament on heresy ... as shown publicly when a certain Rogers was burnt yesterday. Some of the onlookers wept, others prayed to God to give him strength, perseverance and patience to bear the pain and not to recant, others gathered the ashes and bones and wrapped them up in paper to preserve them, yet others threatening the bishops. The haste with which the bishops have proceeded in this matter may well cause a revolt ...

(a) How useful is this extract as evidence of the reaction of people to the burning of heretics in Mary's reign?

(b) To what extent does it agree or disagree on this aspect with the account of the death of Cranmer in Foxe's *Book of Martyrs* (pages 41–42)?

2 Mary acquired the nickname 'Bloody Mary' long after her death. Divide a page into two columns. On the left-hand side write down arguments that justify the nickname of 'Bloody Mary' and on the right-hand side, any arguments that suggest she does not deserve the title. In your opinion, does she deserve the name?

3 Explain how successful Thomas Cranmer was as a Church leader.

Exercise 3.5

SOURCE A: An account of Cranmer's last moments in 1556, by The Rev. E. Hirst in an article published in 1934.

His humiliation was now turned into a triumph. Out of his misery he rose like the true man he was. Bound to the stake after he himself had stripped off his upper garments, he saw the flames lighted, and thrusting his right hand into the fire, the hand which had signed his recantation, he said with a loud voice, 'This hand hath offended.' The burning of his hand first was his own voluntary recantation of those recantations which had been drawn from him by falsehood and trickery when his body was weakened by confinement in prison, and by persistent persecution. Thus, he died, a martyr for truth, suffering for his opinions. His death was no defeat. It was a victory.

SOURCE B: An account of the public reaction to burnings, from *English Reformations* by Christopher Haigh, published in 1993.

There was sympathy from the crowds for the great Protestant pastors; when Cardmaker [a Protestant priest] was executed on 30th May 1555, some cried, 'The Lord strengthen thee Cardmaker! The Lord Jesus Christ receive thy spirit!' As six from the Colchester area died outside the town on 2nd July 1557, a large crowd called 'The Lord strengthen them! The Lord comfort them! The Lord pour his mercies upon them!'

SOURCE C: The burning of three Guernsey martyrs, from Foxe's *Book of Martyrs*, 1563.

■ The burning of three Guernsey martyrs – Foxe's *Book of Martyrs*, 1563

3 Edward VI and Mary I

1   What can you learn from Source A about Thomas Cranmer's death?

2   How far do Sources A and B agree on the extent to which the burning of Protestants was seen as acts of martyrdom?

3   How useful is Source C to a historian studying the persecution of Protestants in Mary's reign?

4   Using all the sources and your own knowledge, how far do you agree with the view that Protestantism had become more popular than Catholicism by the end of Mary's reign?

Exercise 3.6

To answer the following questions, you may need to do some research of your own.

1   Foxe's *Book of Martyrs* was published in 1563 during the reign of Elizabeth I and was intended to justify the condemnation of Catholics. To what extent is it a useful source for historians studying the reign of Queen Mary?

2   More Protestants were burnt in London, Kent, Sussex and Essex during Mary's reign than in the rest of the country put together. Can you think why this might have been?

3   The vast majority of Protestants burnt by Mary were craftsmen and merchants, rather than rich nobles. Can you explain this?

Elizabeth I, 1558–1603

Early life

Elizabeth was born in 1533, the daughter of Henry VIII and Anne Boleyn. Like her half-sister Mary, she had a troubled childhood. In 1536, her mother was executed, charged with adultery and accused of being a witch; Elizabeth herself was declared illegitimate.

Although Elizabeth was not the son her father had hoped for, she was highly intelligent, schooled in Latin, French, Italian and Spanish, and was both musical and artistic. She loved dancing, and played the virginals, a keyboard instrument rather like a harpsichord, and the lute. A devout Protestant, she lived in relative comfort while her brother Edward was king, but when her Catholic sister Mary came to the throne she was imprisoned, briefly, in the Tower of London, before being transferred to Woodstock after Wyatt's Rebellion, where she continued to live, never quite sure of her own safety.

■ Elizabeth I playing the lute; from a portrait painted in c.1580 by Nicholas Hilliard

Problems facing Elizabeth

On her accession to the throne in November 1558, Elizabeth faced troubled times ahead. As Armagil Waad, the Clerk of the Privy Council, wrote, the situation was bleak:

The Queen poor, the realm exhausted, the nobility poor and decayed. The people out of order. Justice not executed. All things expensive. Divisions among ourselves. Wars with France and Scotland.

Elizabeth faced four main problems:

The possibility of invasion

The first problem for Elizabeth was the threat of invasion. There was a real danger that the French might attack England.

The French King Francis claimed that Elizabeth, whom some Roman Catholics saw as illegitimate, had no right to the throne. He claimed that the only marriage of Henry VIII that was recognised in the eyes of God was the one with Catherine of Aragon. Now that the only child of that marriage, Mary, was dead, the throne should pass to the nearest legitimate descendant of Henry VII: none other than Francis's wife, Mary, Queen of Scots. Although Francis died in 1560, the threat from France was never far away.

Religious divisions

A second problem was that the country was divided by religious differences. The people of England had lived through three reigns of religious upheaval, and had witnessed burnings and persecution on a scale never seen before, all in the name of religion. Some of her subjects were still ardent Roman Catholics, some were ardent Protestants. The majority, in all likelihood, were deeply confused by the upheavals of the previous reigns, and probably just wished to be allowed to go to church, say their prayers, and get on with their lives as their fathers and grandfathers had before them. Elizabeth herself was a Protestant, but she wished to establish a religious settlement that would be as inclusive as possible. As she said: 'I do not seek a window into men's souls.'

Legitimacy, marriage and gender

As we have seen, the King of France claimed that Elizabeth had no right to be queen because she was illegitimate. Those who agreed with him, who upheld the Catholic view that Henry VIII's marriage to Catherine of Aragon had never, rightly, been annulled, thus posed a threat to her rule. The surest way to overcome this threat was to marry and secure a legitimate heir of her own. Indeed, as a woman, it was assumed that she would marry, women not being considered capable of ruling on their own (the recent example of Mary had not been a success!). But this in turn led to concerns that whoever she married would be bound to reduce England to the status of a puppet state.

Money

Finally, Elizabeth faced money problems. The government was short of money when she became queen and, for a country possibly facing a foreign invasion, this was a serious concern. Poor harvests had caused starvation and famine, the enclosure laws were unpopular, and an ever-increasing number of paupers and beggars, who might in an earlier age have found refuge in one of the monasteries, roamed the streets. Money was to remain a source of concern to Elizabeth for the rest of her life.

The Elizabethan Settlement, 1559

Perhaps the most urgent of these problems facing Elizabeth was religion. She was a moderate Protestant, but she knew that many of her subjects were more extreme Protestants, while others favoured Roman Catholic doctrines and papal authority. Elizabeth set out to devise a religious policy that would avoid offending too many and that could be accepted by the majority of the English people.

In 1559, Elizabeth created a Church system, referred to as the Elizabethan Settlement, which was Protestant and based on the twin pillars of the Acts of Supremacy and Uniformity. This was the beginnings of what became known as the Anglican Church.

1 By the Act of Supremacy, Elizabeth became the Supreme Governor of the Church of England and papal authority was, once more, abolished. In effect, Elizabeth restored the situation which her father had established and which her sister had reversed.

2 By the Act of Uniformity, the 1552 *Book of Common Prayer*, together with elements of the 1549 Prayer Book, was reinstated and its use made compulsory by all clergy. The clothing or vestments worn by the clergy, and the ornamentation of the churches, was to be as laid down in the 1549 Prayer Book. Those refusing to accept these pronouncements would be removed from office. Attendance at church on Sundays and holy days was made compulsory. Failure to do so would lead to fines called recusancy fines.

There were some striking compromises in the Elizabethan Settlement. A good example of this is in the part of the communion service dealing with the distribution of the bread and wine. Elizabeth's amalgamation of the earlier Prayer Books seemed to allow two if not three interpretations: the idea for example that the bread did indeed become the actual body of Christ; the idea that this only happened for those who truly believed in Him; and the idea that it was simply a commemoration of Christ's presence.

Another important compromise was the wording in the Act of Supremacy, which made Elizabeth, not Supreme Head, but Supreme Governor of the Church of England. It was a subtle difference, but just enough to placate those who still really thought that the Pope should be head of the Church.

She also wanted to create a Church hierarchy that rejected the really radical Protestant ideas, so replaced those bishops who had resigned with moderates and appointed the moderate Matthew Parker as Archbishop of Canterbury.

Elizabeth knew that neither extreme Protestants nor extreme Roman Catholics would be likely to accept the settlement, but she wanted to find a compromise for as many people as possible.

The Anglican Church, or Church of England, eventually spread around the world. In which countries might you find large numbers of Anglican churches today? Why do you think Anglicanism spread to these particular countries?

The Thirty-Nine Articles

In 1563, the Church agreed to the Thirty-Nine Articles. These were based upon Cranmer's Forty-Two Articles of 1553 and established Elizabeth's Church as moderately Protestant. They were passed by Parliament in 1571. They condemned some Catholic practices, such as transubstantiation and the cult of the Virgin Mary. They also supported key Protestant teachings, for example, the importance of the Bible, the giving of both bread and wine to everybody at communion, and allowing the clergy to marry. In 1560 Elizabeth had accepted the dedication to her of a new English translation of the Bible, the Geneva (or 'Breeches') Bible, and this was distributed and widely used.

Elizabeth and the Puritans

As we have seen, Elizabeth was willing to accommodate both Catholics and Protestants but was determined to stamp down on extremists of either type. The extreme Protestants became known as Puritans, because of their desire to purify the Church.

The teachings of Luther, and then the more radical Calvin, had led to the Protestant Church's rejection of the Pope as head of the Church, and a questioning of the fundamental importance of priests in Christianity. The most extreme Protestants, or Puritans, wished to take this even further and dispense with bishops altogether. Inspired by the publication in 1563 of the fiercely anti-Catholic *Acts and Monuments* (also known as Foxe's *Book of Martyrs*), the Puritans hoped to push Elizabeth towards a more extreme form of Protestantism. In 1571, following a series of Puritan lectures given at Cambridge University by Thomas Cartwright the previous year, Puritan MPs tried to make the Prayer Book more radical. Heated debates followed between Archbishop Parker and the Puritan leaders and in 1574, the Puritans published their own alternative Prayer Book.

The next year, Parker died. Elizabeth appointed a famous Protestant preacher named Edmund Grindal to be the new Archbishop of Canterbury but he proved incapable of standing up to the Puritans and she suspended him from his duties in 1577 after he refused to ban Puritan 'prophesyings' (meetings at which Puritan ministers debated the meaning of Biblical readings in front of large crowds).

When Grindal died in 1583, John Whitgift was appointed Archbishop of Canterbury. By the end of Elizabeth's reign, however, the Puritan problem had still not gone away – and was to re-emerge a few decades later in an even more extreme form.

Elizabeth and the Catholics

At the other religious extreme, Catholics also posed a major threat to Elizabeth, not least because they had powerful allies overseas in Philip II of Spain and the King of France. As in her dealings with the Puritans, Elizabeth's attitude was that her Church should be able to include moderate Catholics, but a small number of extreme Catholics pushed her to the limit. We will examine these in more detail later:

1 When Mary Queen of Scots arrived in England in 1568 (see page 53), she quickly became the focus of Catholic plots against Elizabeth. Mary had a claim to the throne through her grandmother (see the family tree on page 162) and some Catholics considered her to be the true Queen of England because they believed Elizabeth was illegitimate.
2 The Northern Rebellion (see page 53) in 1569 and Pope Pius V's excommunication of Elizabeth in 1570 worsened the situation. By excommunicating her, and calling upon all good Catholics to disobey her, Pius V was effectively ordering her subjects to disown her as queen.
3 The Duke of Norfolk, one of the leading nobles in England, was also plotting against Elizabeth at this point. The Ridolfi Plot of 1571 (see page 53) led to Norfolk's arrest and execution in 1572.

To deal with these threats, in 1573 Elizabeth placed a minor knight named Sir Francis Walsingham in charge of security. He carefully monitored any Catholic plots using a wide and ruthless network of spies. Meanwhile Jesuits, Catholic priests who had been trained overseas, started appearing in England and staying undercover with rich Catholic families in false lofts, priest-holes and cellars. Despite the fact that the fine for Catholics who refused to go to church on Sunday was increased in 1581 to £20 per month, Catholicism continued to flourish.

William Cecil, Lord Burghley

To help her through all these problems, Elizabeth relied on William Cecil, who had previously served both Edward and Mary, and who was appointed Secretary of State in 1558 and became Lord Treasurer in 1572. Cecil helped reduce government spending and encouraged exploration to find new markets for English goods (see pages 68–69). Elizabeth rewarded him in 1571 by making him Lord Burghley (the only one of her ministers to be ennobled) and trusted him completely. She said of him:

This judgment I have of you, that you will not be corrupted with any manner of gifts, and that you will be faithful to the state.

One of Cecil's greatest skills was his ability to be Elizabeth's spokesman in Parliament, while at the same time keeping Elizabeth in touch with Parliament's moods and attitudes. Aware that wars were very expensive, he also proved a cautious advisor on foreign policy. He made sure England's defences were organised and modernised, so that any potential foreign invasion could be repelled. Whereas men close to the Queen such as the dashing Earl of Leicester may have amused her, and while Francis Walsingham and others urged policies dictated by their own religious beliefs, Cecil was always careful and considered in his advice. Nevertheless, he was determined that never again would there be a Catholic monarch on the English throne, and so was keener than Elizabeth to take action against Mary Queen of Scots. Elizabeth relied heavily on Cecil and called him 'my spirit'. It is said that she fed him by hand during his final days. He died in 1598 and his son Robert Cecil succeeded him as Secretary. William's advice to his son was interesting: 'Serve God by serving of the Queen, for all other service is bondage to the Devil'.

■ William Cecil, Lord Burghley; a portrait painted in the sixteenth century by Arnold von Brounckhorst

Exercise 4.1

1 Create four lists where the heading of each is one of the problems Elizabeth I faced when she became Queen of England. Underneath each heading write several points about why each problem was important.

2 Explain which was the most difficult problem Elizabeth I faced when she became Queen of England.

Mary Stuart, Queen of Scots

Mary was the daughter of James V, King of Scotland. She was born in 1542 and became queen the same year on the death of her father. She was brought up in France, and in 1558 was married to Francis, the heir to the French throne. However, it was a short marriage: Francis became king in 1559 but died of an ear infection a year later, and Mary returned to Scotland a widow in 1561.

The death of Rizzio

In 1565, Mary married her cousin, Henry, Lord Darnley. Darnley was a bully, and Mary soon turned to her Italian secretary, David Rizzio, for comfort. Darnley was furious and ordered Rizzio's murder.

On 9 March 1566, Mary was having a meal with Rizzio and her ladies-in-waiting when they were interrupted by Darnley and several men. Mary was threatened at gunpoint and Rizzio was seized and dragged away. He was brutally thrown down a flight of stairs, stripped of his clothes and jewellery, and killed. It is said that he was stabbed 57 times.

■ Mary believed that the murder of her advisor, Rizzio, was an attempt to make her miscarry her unborn child and die

The death of Darnley

Mary and Darnley were superficially reconciled, and in June 1566 they had a son, James. But it was not to last, and Mary now turned to another lover, the Earl of Bothwell. A year later, Darnley died in mysterious circumstances, when the house where he was staying in Edinburgh was destroyed by an explosion and his body was discovered some distance from the house, in an orchard. It appeared at first that he had been trying to escape the explosion, but when he was found to have been strangled, suspicion fell on Bothwell.

Bothwell was tried and found not guilty and, three months later, he and Mary were married. The people were outraged and rebellion broke out. Mary was seized, imprisoned in Lochleven Castle and forced to give up the throne to her son, James. On 2 May 1568, she cut off her red hair so no one would recognise her, escaped from the castle dressed as a maid, and headed for England.

Mary sought refuge with her cousin, Elizabeth, placing Elizabeth in a difficult position. Mary had already made it clear to her cousin that she viewed her claim to the English throne as a strong one. In 1562 she had written to her: 'We know how near we are descended of the

> Look into the circumstances of Darnley's death. Why was it viewed suspiciously? What are the arguments for and against Bothwell being guilty of his murder?

blood of England. We trust, being your cousin, ye would be loth we should receive so manifest an injury as all utterly to be debarred from that title which in possibility may fall unto us.' Elizabeth was naturally wary of Mary, who was at the time a fugitive, suspected of murder, and keen to state her claims to the throne of England. But she was reluctant to harm her. Perhaps her own fears during the reign of her sister, when poor Lady Jane Grey had been executed, influenced her and made her take pity on her cousin.

■ Mary, Queen of Scots arriving at the Tower of London

Either way, Elizabeth did what she did best: she compromised; and for the next nineteen years, Mary was held prisoner.

Catholic plots

Elizabeth's concerns turned out to be well justified, and while Mary was in England she became a focus for those Catholics who wanted to remove Elizabeth from the throne. There were several plots against Elizabeth as a result: the Northern Rebellion in 1569; the Ridolfi Plot in 1571; the Throckmorton Plot in 1583; and the Babington Plot in 1586.

The Northern Rebellion, 1569

One of the country's leading Catholic families was the Howard family, who were Dukes of Norfolk. They wished Elizabeth to recognise Mary's claim to the throne, and to name her as her successor. When in 1569 Elizabeth discovered that there were plans for Mary to marry the Duke of Norfolk, Elizabeth was furious and Norfolk was sent to the Tower of London. This led to an uprising by supporters of the marriage (especially the Earls of Northumberland and Westmorland) who gathered a force of almost 6000 men and secured control of parts of the north-east and much of Yorkshire, hoping that a Spanish force would come to their assistance.

The rebels were challenged by a force under the Earl of Sussex, the President of the Council of the North, and they soon dispersed, with 450 rebels being executed. The Earl of Westmorland escaped to the continent and the Earl of Northumberland fled to Scotland, where he was seized and sold to Elizabeth for £2000. He was interrogated and executed in 1572.

The Ridolfi Plot, 1571

In 1571 Roberto di Ridolfi, a rich Italian banker, plotted to rescue Mary and the Duke of Norfolk from imprisonment and put Mary on the throne. The plot was discovered by Sir Francis Walsingham and Norfolk was executed the following year, which caused Elizabeth anguish because they were related.

The Throckmorton Plot, 1583

England's relations with Spain had deteriorated rapidly after Elizabeth became queen and Philip II of Spain had made clear his wish for Mary Queen of Scots to become ruler of England. In 1583, a Catholic, Francis Throckmorton, took letters apparently written by Mary to the Spanish Ambassador, asking for help. Whether these were genuine or not is unclear, but Sir Francis Walsingham's spies uncovered the plot, and Throckmorton and others were executed. Elizabeth chose not to punish Mary because she lacked sufficient proof that she had been involved in the plot.

The Babington Plot, 1586

Elizabeth had tolerated Mary for many years, but when she was found to have been involved once more in a planned plot against her, Elizabeth ran out of patience. In 1586 Sir Francis Walsingham's spies intercepted letters to Mary from a Catholic, Anthony Babington. The letters were in code and were smuggled in and out of Chartley Hall, Staffordshire, where Mary was being held, in barrels of beer. It seemed from the letters that Babington was plotting to kill Elizabeth and, with assistance from the Spanish, replace her with Mary as queen. Here is an extract from one of Mary's letters to Babington, which was written in code but deciphered by Walsingham:

Long ago, I pointed out to other foreign Catholic princes that the longer we delayed intervening in England, the greater the advantages of our opponents. Meanwhile, the Catholics here, exposed to all kinds of cruelty, steadily grow less in numbers and power. Everything being prepared, and the forces being ready, I must in some way be got from here to await foreign assistance.

Mary was put on trial at Fotheringhay Castle for her part in the Babington plot but the court could not prove that the handwriting was hers. It has been suggested that Walsingham was so determined to implicate Mary that he may have instructed his spies to forge Mary's letter to Babington. He certainly arranged for an extra section to be added to one of Babington's letters to her, asking her to reveal the names of the other conspirators.

Nevertheless, they found her guilty of treason. Elizabeth continued to delay what was surely inevitable, writing to Lord Burghley, 'I pray you to accept my thankfulness, excuse my doubtfulness, and take in good part my answer – answerless.' Eventually she signed a death warrant, but delayed sending it. Burghley himself sent it and Elizabeth later claimed that this had been done against her wishes, and that she had never wanted the death of her cousin. She is reported to have said to the French ambassador:

> *I did indeed sign the warrant; but it was only to satisfy my subjects, as I never intended to put her to death, except in case of a foreign invasion, or a great rebellion of my own subjects. The members of my council have played me a trick which I can never forgive.*

Mary's execution

Whether or not this was true, Mary was executed on 8 February 1587. It took three blows of the executioner's axe to remove her head. Her small pet dog ran terrified underneath the skirts of the body and would not leave her. When the executioner grasped Mary's hair to hold up the head for the spectators to see, Mary's wig came away in his hand and the head fell to the floor. Her real hair was no longer the vivid red of her youth but was now completely grey. Her long life in prison had taken its toll.

Exercise 4.2

1 Write a paragraph or draw a cartoon strip to describe the early life and three marriages of Mary Queen of Scots.

2 Explain why Mary Queen of Scots was a threat to Elizabeth I.

War with Spain

When Elizabeth became queen in 1558, she seriously considered an offer of marriage from Philip II of Spain. By 1588, however, England and Spain were at war: the culmination of three decades of religious, political and imperial rivalry between the two countries.

Religious rivalry

England, under Elizabeth, was a Protestant country and Spain was Catholic. Protestants in Spain were seen as heretics, agents of the devil, and were burnt at the stake. Philip II, who had been married to Elizabeth's sister 'Bloody Mary', the fanatical Catholic, felt it his duty to restore his wife's country to Catholicism when the Protestant Elizabeth came to the throne. The easiest route to this, he thought, was to marry Elizabeth, and in 1559 he proposed marriage but was refused.

Eleven years later, in 1570, when the Pope excommunicated Elizabeth, Philip considered it his duty to overthrow her, and the

Spanish were known to be interested, if not actively involved, in the various plots to put Mary Queen of Scots on the throne. For her part, Elizabeth lent her support to Protestants rebelling against Spanish rule in the Netherlands in 1572, and in 1585 she sent an army under the Earl of Leicester to help the Dutch Protestants in their fight against Philip.

Political rivalry

The rivalry between England and Spain was not just religious. There was also political rivalry between the two countries. In 1579 Elizabeth considered a marriage alliance with the Duke of Alençon, heir to the French throne and a bitter enemy of Philip's. In 1580, England signed a trade treaty with the Turks, who were enemies of Spain. In the same year, when Philip conquered Portugal, Elizabeth promised to help the rival claimant to the throne, Dom Antonio, in his fight against Philip.

Imperial rivalry

Finally, there was imperial rivalry between England and Spain. Spain had control of the New World (Central and South America) and had a lucrative trade there, in items such as slaves and gold, which England was threatening. English ships were engaged in transporting slaves from Africa to these colonies in breach of Philip's orders that only Spanish ships could trade with the New World. In 1568, three Spanish treasure ships, sheltering from a storm in Southampton, were seized by Elizabeth. The next year, the seafaring adventurer Francis Drake raided Spanish ships and took South American treasure back to Elizabeth. Drake was considered a pirate by Philip, so when he returned to England in 1580 after successfully sailing around the world, Philip was furious to hear that Elizabeth had knighted him.

The Spanish Armada, 1588

The execution of Mary Queen of Scots in 1587 provided a convenient excuse for Philip. Mary would almost certainly have been an ally of France, not Spain, if she had become Queen of England, but her death as a Catholic martyr gave Philip more open cause to attack Protestant England. In fact, preparations for an invasion of England had been going on since 1586.

Singeing the King of Spain's beard

Drake, sent to the coast of Spain with a fleet to disrupt any moves to create a fleet that might attack England or Ireland, launched a daring raid into the harbour at Cadiz. He set fire to a number of ships which then drifted onto other Spanish vessels. The flames spread, and around 30 Spanish warships and vessels were destroyed, along with valuable supplies. This action, referred to as 'the singeing of the King of Spain's beard', delayed the Spanish preparations. Philip dismissed it as not serious, but stated that 'their audacity is intolerable'.

Drake and the game of bowls

In 1588, plans for the invasion were finally complete. Philip gathered an army of 30 000 in the Netherlands and the plan was to send a huge armada (fleet) of ships to guard and assist the army as it crossed to England. But there were problems with supplies and the first attempt to sail in May was stopped by storms. Philip also had problems in choosing a man of high enough rank to command, eventually deciding upon the Duke of Medina Sidonia. The Duke had no sailing experience but was an excellent organiser, and was to prove both a good leader and brave. On 22 July, 130 ships set sail from Corunna, reaching the Channel on 30 July.

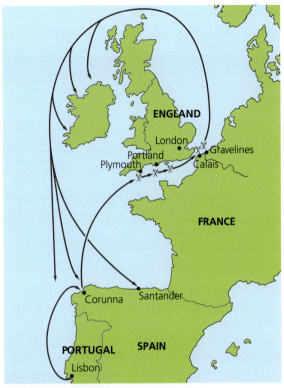
■ The route of the Spanish Armada, 1588

Drake, we are told, was playing a game of bowls on Plymouth Hoe when the Armada was first spotted. On being warned about the approach of the Spanish fleet, Drake is said to have remarked that there was plenty of time to finish the game of bowls and still beat the Spaniards. Although this sounds wonderfully relaxed and self-confident, it may simply have been that he knew he had to wait for the tide before he could put out to sea.

The first battles

When the English fleet at Plymouth sailed out to meet the Spanish the Armada formed a defensive 'half moon' formation, or crescent, which the English had not seen before. The heavier and slower Spanish cargo ships, called hulks, were placed in the middle of the crescent and protected by some of the galleons (warships). Other galleons and four special vessels called galleasses, which used both oars and sails, were located at the two ends of the crescent, nearest the pursuing English fleet. The English wanted to use their advantage of quicker, more manoeuvrable ships and longer-range cannon. Lord Howard made an attempt to attack the Armada off Plymouth on Sunday 31 July. Neither side caused any real damage before the English fell back. The only two Spanish losses during this period were because of accidents. One ship collided with another, fell behind and was captured by Drake. Another had an explosion on board and was picked up by the English.

The English Fleet	The Spanish Armada
197 ships scattered in ports in the south of England	130 ships
34 war galleons (30 146 tonnes)	22 war galleons (58 408 tonnes)
15 000 men	30 000 men
Some new, redesigned, fast warships	Larger, much slower warships
Bold commanders such as Drake and Hawkins under the command of Lord Howard of Effingham, the Queen's first cousin.	The Spanish commander, the Duke of Medina Sidonia, had no experience of commanding a fleet but had veteran commanders such as Juan Martínez de Recalde.

As the fleets sailed the English were reinforced by more ships from Portsmouth. But off Portland Bill on Tuesday 2 August it appears that the Spanish were the attackers and there was a sharp fight for several hours. Again and again the Spanish ships attempted to come alongside the English in order to use the large number of Spanish soldiers on their ships to board the lower-built English ships. But the quicker English ships were able to move away and tried to use their cannon to disable the Spanish ships. At the end of the fight neither side was much hurt, although the English were becoming concerned about their ammunition supply. Lord Howard had already sent this message to shore, 'For the love of God and the country, let us have with some speed some great shot sent us of all bigness; for this service will continue long; and some powder with it.'

The third battle occurred off the Isle of Wight on 3 and 4 August. The English believed this is where the Spanish meant to land and closed on the Armada, but the winds were so light that some ships had to be towed into battle. Again, neither side caused much damage and the Armada continued to sail towards its meeting with Parma and his army in what is today Belgium.

The fact was that even though the battles off the south coast of England had not stopped the Armada, the Spanish plan had already failed. Its weakness from the start had been that there was no method for the fleet to co-ordinate its timings with Parma's army. Many of the Spanish commanders knew what they were attempting was virtually impossible. Juan Martínez de Recalde had stated, 'Unless God helps us with a miracle the English, who have faster and handier ships than ours, and many more long-range guns … will never close with us at all, but stand off and knock us to pieces with their cannons, without our being able to do them any serious hurt. So we are sailing against England in the confident hope of a miracle.'

Fireships off Calais

Medina Sidonia ordered the Armada to anchor off the French port of Calais on Saturday 6 August. It was while waiting here that he received word that Parma would not be able to send his army out into the Channel in its fleet of small ships and barges for maybe as long as a fortnight. With the English fleet anchored nearby and Calais a poor anchorage, with its swift currents and openness to storms, the Spanish commanders were very unhappy, but decided for the moment to stay. The English, however, had other plans.

■ The English sent fireships into the midst of the Spanish fleet

On the night of Sunday 7 August, Lord Howard felt he had to take action. His ships had suffered little damage but disease was beginning to reduce his crews. He chose eight ships from the fleet and allowed them to drift with the tide down on to the anchored Spanish. These were **fireships**, filled with flammable materials and set alight as they closed with the Spanish ships. Even though the Spanish had small boats out and towed several of the burning ships away, others drifted through towards the fleet. The Spanish had no choice but to cut their anchor ropes and sail north, breaking their formation.

Gravelines and the flight of the Armada

The next day found the Armada scattered in the English Channel and the English fleet rapidly approaching. Medina Sidonia turned his and a handful of other Spanish ships to fight the English while the rest of his fleet re-gathered. This battle off Gravelines was to be the longest and bloodiest of the whole Armada campaign. The Spanish were to lose several ships, including the galleass *San Lorenzo* grounded off Calais. The English managed to come closer to the Spanish than ever before and there are reports of blood draining from the scuppers, or drains, of some Spanish ships. The *San Martin*, Medina Sidonia's flagship, was reckoned by one of its officers to have been hit more than 200 times by cannon fire. Drake led an attack on the flagship, turned his line of ships around and gave the *San Martin* another broadside.

One of the English commanders, John Hawkins, described events in a letter sent to the Queen's Secretary after the battle:

All that day we followed the Spaniards with a long and great fight, wherein there was great valour showed generally by our company. Our ships, God be thanked, have received little hurt, though some have need of repair of sail and rigging.

Incredibly, the Spanish crescent reformed and the Armada sailed further north, away from Parma and his army. Unable to turn and fight his way back to Parma, Medina Sidonia ordered his fleet to make its way back home sailing around the British Isles. The English fleet followed for several days, then returned back to port.

The Spanish had little food left and many of the sailors and soldiers were sick or wounded. Storms split up the Armada, and many of the ships were so badly damaged by the fighting that they simply disappeared, sunk with all hands. Several other ships were captured by the Dutch, who kept the Spanish officers for ransom and drowned the rest of the crews. A number of ships crashed upon the shores of Scotland or Ireland and the English garrison of Ireland, in great fear of large numbers of shipwrecked Spaniards, massacred many of those they took prisoner. Eventually 90 ships of the Armada returned to Spain. Of the missing 60 only four are known to have been captured by the English or sunk in battle. Twenty-five are known to have been wrecked off the coast of Ireland. Some 11 000 Spanish sailors and soldiers had died. The Duke of Medina Sidonia was so weak that he had to be carried home, and his career was ruined. Juan Martínez de Recalde died four days after guiding his ship back to Spain.

> Research the casualties of the Spanish Armada. What were the losses in battle, and which were due to shipwrecks and storms? Can the Spanish be said to have truly been 'defeated' by the English?

Results of the Armada

Although the Spanish Armada was defeated, the war against Spain continued. For nearly two months after losing sight of the Spanish, the English fleet was kept in harbour, ready to fight again. It was not until late September that Elizabeth's government was sure that the threat was finally over. By that time about half the English sailors of the fleet were dead. Only about 100 Englishmen were hurt during the battles of the Armada, but the sickness that had worried Lord Howard off Calais had devastated the fleet, made worse by Elizabeth's government's failure to pay its sailors.

Following the defeat of the Spanish Armada, Elizabeth's popularity was at an all-time high, and she was not slow to use the defeat of the Armada in her propaganda. The portrait of Elizabeth shown here, for example, shows her as mistress of land and sea. Her fingers are touching America on the globe, and the image of the defeated Armada in the background celebrates one of the greatest triumphs of her reign.

■ Elizabeth I; from a painting attributed to George Gower produced around 1588, known as the 'Armada Portrait'

Philip continued to plot to bring England to heel and several more Armadas were prepared, although they were never successfully launched. In 1589 Sir Francis Drake was involved in a disastrous attack on Portugal, leaving his reputation in tatters, and other attempts to attack Spanish possessions or capture her treasure galleons all failed. However, at the end of Elizabeth's reign, England remained a Protestant country, free of Spain.

Exercise 4.3

1 Draw a timeline from 1559–87. On the timeline, plot the main events that brought England and Spain to war.

2 Explain the causes of the war between England and Spain during the reign of Elizabeth I.

3 Explain why the Spanish Armada of 1588 was defeated.

You may find it useful to fill in the table below.

Actions, strengths and weaknesses of the English	Actions, strengths and weaknesses of the Spanish

Wars in Ireland

With the direct threat from Spain at an end, Elizabeth now faced trouble in Ireland. For over 200 years, English kings had claimed authority over Ireland, but in reality royal control was very limited. In most of the country, the local Irish nobles exercised power and it was only in the area around Dublin, known as the **Pale**, that Elizabeth's officials had any control. Furthermore, Ireland had remained Catholic, little affected by the religious upheaval of the past 50 years, and as such was a potential base from which Catholic countries could invade Protestant England.

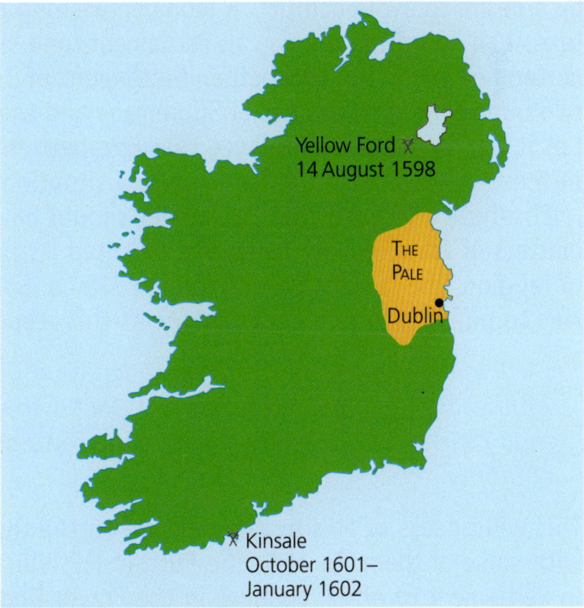

The most serious challenge to Elizabeth's authority in Ireland came from Hugh O'Neill, the Earl of Tyrone, who constantly challenged her power and, in 1598, at the head of an army of 6000 men, defeated a small English force at the Battle of the Yellow Ford. This victory allowed

Yellow Ford ✗
14 August 1598

THE
PALE

Dublin

✗ Kinsale
October 1601–
January 1602

■ The Pale and the wars in Ireland

Tyrone to impose his rule across much of Ireland, and forced Elizabeth to take action.

In 1599 she sent her favourite, the dashing Earl of Essex, to put down Tyrone's rebellion, but the campaign was a disaster. She replaced Essex with the much more competent commander, Lord Mountjoy, and this time her troops were successful. In a series of battles at Kinsale on the southern tip of Ireland, Tyrone was defeated, together with a force of 4000 Spanish who had been sent in support of this Catholic challenge to Elizabeth. Tyrone was forced to surrender and in 1603 he swore loyalty to Elizabeth.

The fall of Essex

One unexpected result of Elizabeth's wars in Ireland was the fall of her one-time favourite, the Earl of Essex. Essex was humiliated by his failure in Ireland and had returned to England without permission. He blamed Elizabeth's ministers for turning the Queen against him. On 8 February 1601 he raised a force in London but again proved his own incompetence. Few people joined him and he was soon afterwards arrested and executed for treason. This showed that Elizabeth put her throne and country ahead of her personal feelings.

Elizabeth and Parliament

As in so many areas, Elizabeth's dealings with Parliament were governed by a desire to avoid conflict. A monarch wishing to pass laws or raise taxes had no option but to call Parliament, and she did so ten times during her reign. The Elizabethan Settlement of 1559 rested on the two important acts, the Act of Supremacy and the Act of Uniformity, but it was in the area of finance that Elizabeth found herself becoming increasingly dependent on Parliament, a situation she bitterly resented.

Elizabeth conceded that Parliament should have the right to discuss matters of state, but in reality she resented its interference in matters of religion, the succession and foreign affairs. She also refused to allow MPs to put pressure on her to marry, as this response clearly shows:

I will marry as soon as I can conveniently; if God take him not away with whom I had a mind to marry ... but I shall do no otherwise than pleases me. Your bills can have no force without my assent and authority.

This willingness of MPs to put pressure on the Queen led to conflict with some of them. In 1571 the Puritan MP William Strickland tried in Parliament to effect changes in the Prayer Book. He was rudely rebuffed. In 1572 Peter Wentworth, another Puritan, criticised Elizabeth for not consulting Parliament on her plans, but rather leaking these through her officials. He was arrested and thrown into the Tower.

In 1587, Anthony Cope tried to use Parliament to get approval for a series of Puritan amendments to the Prayer Book. Again, Elizabeth managed to resist, but she was furious that her authority had been challenged and ordered the arrest of several of the MPs concerned.

Other political issues were also debated in Parliament, ranging from the succession to the throne to what to do with Mary Queen of Scots. Parliament also passed a number of Acts regarding poor relief and the problem of beggars (see page 72). Subsidies (taxes paid to the monarch) were debated and agreed to several times, although the debates became more divisive later in Elizabeth's reign when the country's economy started to experience problems. In 1596, for example, Parliament kept the Queen waiting for 24 days while it debated whether or not to grant her a tax to pay for the ongoing war with Spain.

On balance, though, Elizabeth's handling of Parliament was generally very astute and she prided herself on her good relations with it. This is borne out in her last address to Parliament in 1601, the so-called 'Golden Speech', when she claimed proudly:

Though God hath raised me high, yet this I count the glory of my crown, that I have reigned with your loves.

Elizabeth and imagery

We have seen how Elizabeth used the portrait on page 60 to celebrate her victory over the Spanish Armada and to point to future colonial expansion in the Americas. This use of portraiture as propaganda was a continuation of what we have already seen in the portraits, for example, of her father Henry VIII; but Elizabeth took this to a new level. Elizabeth, as a woman, was deeply aware of the need to promote an image of herself which counteracted any perceived weakness in her sex. She did this by deliberately cultivating an image of herself as regal, beautiful, confident and virginal, and regularly she portrayed herself as a bringer of peace. In the so-called 'Pelican portrait' attributed to Nicholas Hilliard (c.1575) her claim to the throne of France is marked by the fleur de lys, and the pelican pendant she is wearing represents her self-sacrifice (the pelican is famous in legend for having pricked its own breast to feed its young with blood).

In another portrait, by Marcus Gheeraerts the Elder (c.1580), the Queen is represented as the bringer of peace, with an olive branch

■ Elizabeth I; from a painting often attributed to Isaac Oliver produced around 1600; today this is known as the 'Rainbow Portrait'

in her hand and a sheathed sword at her feet. In one by Quentin Metsys the Younger (c.1583), she is represented holding a sieve, the symbol of chastity and purity, and is also linked to the Roman hero Aeneas, who, like her, had rejected marriage (to Dido) in favour of fulfilling his destiny and mission to rebuild his nation. Similarly, the famous 'Rainbow portrait' (on page 63) is full of imagery. Elizabeth is depicted as Astraea, the star-maiden, the daughter of Zeus who represented the end of the Golden Age in Greek mythology before the fall of man, and who was to be transformed into the star Virgo. Her crown is encrusted with rubies and pearls, the symbol of virginity, and the crescent-shaped jewel above her crown links her to the moon. The serpent, representing wisdom, and the heart-shaped ruby, representing the Queen's heart, are deliberately linked. Finally, the rainbow, and the inscription *non sine sole iris* (no rainbow without the sun), are powerful reminders that Elizabeth is the regal bringer of peace.

> Find copies of the portraits mentioned above. From all you know about Elizabeth I, which portrait do you think is the most effective at portraying her personality?

Elizabeth's achievements

Elizabeth died in 1603, unmarried and childless. After her death she became known as 'Good Queen Bess'; but how successful was she?

Elizabeth had ruled for 45 years, a woman in a largely male world. She had carefully cultivated the image of the 'Virgin Queen', reminding people that her duty to her country came before marriage, and provided a long period of much-needed stability after the troubled reigns of Edward and Mary. Her navy had successfully repelled the threat of invasion from Spain, she had defeated Catholic plots in England, often revolving round Mary Queen of Scots, and had brought some form of control over Ireland. Moreover, she had settled the religious issue with a policy of moderate Protestantism, and created the Anglican Church, which is still in existence today. As we will see in the next chapter, her Poor Laws remained the basis for government policy toward beggars and the poor for over 200 years.

Despite occasional criticism, Parliament was a loyal supporter of Elizabeth, and the absence of any truly serious rebellions demonstrates the extent of support for the monarch.

However, there were problems and failures. By the 1590s, the economy began to falter; there were several poor harvests and the country was frequently beset by unrest. The Poor Laws did nothing to tackle the economic and social problems of the 1590s, which led to much poverty. Despite her moderate religious settlement, Puritans and Catholics remained hostile to the Church of England. In addition, by her growing need to call Parliament to fund her war with Spain, she raised the expectations of Parliament and the status of MPs. Elizabeth, by accident, created the impression that there was more of a partnership between Crown and Parliament than actually existed.

All of these things were to cause problems for her Stuart successors. And finally, by her refusal to marry, she failed to resolve the problem of who would succeed her.

Exercise 4.4

1 Explain how successful Elizabeth I was in her dealings with Parliament.

2 Draw up a balance sheet of Elizabeth's achievements. On the left-hand side list her successes or strengths, on the right-hand side, her failures or shortcomings. Explain what you think was Elizabeth's greatest achievement.

3 Look at the 'Rainbow portrait' on page 63. Why do you think Elizabeth was portrayed in this way? You might like to consider the imagery of the rainbow, the serpent, the pearls, the eyes and ears; the size and flamboyance of her clothes; and the apparent age of the Queen in the portrait.

4 Explain how successful Elizabeth I was as Queen of England.

5 Life in the sixteenth century

◯ Enclosure

The later fifteenth and early sixteenth centuries were a time of great change in England, not least in the area of agriculture. For hundreds of years peasant farmers had ploughed strips of land on their feudal lord's manor, but increasingly landowners were turning to sheep farming instead of arable farming. The wool trade was making landowners and merchants rich, and returns from wool greatly outstripped those from corn. Sheep farming was less labour intensive, and required land to be enclosed which previously had been open fields. Both of these factors caused hardship to the poor peasant farmers, who relied on the land for their livelihood.

■ The enclosures meant poverty for many peasant farmers

There were two features of enclosure. First, there was the enclosure of open fields. These open fields had previously been divided up into strips, each of which was rented by a farmer. By enclosing these fields, and turning them over to pasture for sheep, landowners cut these peasant farmers off from the land they had worked on for generations.

Secondly, there was the enclosure of the common land. Every village had a stretch of land on which the villagers grazed their animals and poultry (chickens and geese). When this land was fenced off by the local landowner and used for private pasture, it caused great hardship, as this letter from the Bishop of Lincoln to Cardinal Wolsey in September 1530 shows:

Your heart should mourn to see the towns, villages, hamlets and manor places, in ruin and decay, the people gone, the ploughs laid down, the living of many honest men in one man's hand, the commons in many places taken away from the poor people, so that they are compelled to give up their houses and know not where to live.

Understandably, reaction to enclosure was often violent. Mobs tore down the fences, walls and hedges. Petitions were collected and angry crowds, such as the men who followed Kett's Rebellion in 1549, gathered together in an effort to make the government aware of their grievances. Efforts were made to limit the hardships brought about by enclosure, but these were largely ineffective, as the local government officials entrusted with looking into abuses, the Justices of the Peace (JPs), often owned enclosures themselves. Certainly, when Cardinal Wolsey attempted to end the practice of enclosure in some places during the 1520s, this aroused considerable opposition from the aristocracy and gentry who benefited so much from the process of enclosure.

It is also true that the enclosure movement stimulated the growth of the woollen industry and therefore increased government tax revenues from export sales. Because English merchants initially lacked the expertise to make finished cloth, wool was sent to the towns of Flanders in the Netherlands to be made into textiles. Until 1558, wool had to be exported through the 'staple' port of Calais (under English control until that date), and government officials taxed the wool as it passed through. Enclosing the land led to more wool being exported, and thus more money being raised in taxes.

Exercise 5.1

1 Copy and complete the following table.

Causes of enclosure	Process of enclosure	Results of enclosure

2 Explain how enclosure affected ordinary people in England during the sixteenth century.

The growth of trade

The Tudor period saw a huge growth in trade as England's economy moved, very slowly, from agriculture, with wealth coming largely from the land, to commerce, with wealth stemming from trade in manufactured goods. England began to develop industries, often localised, such as the following:

- cast iron from Kent
- coal from Newcastle
- copper from Cumbria
- lead from Somerset
- salt from Cheshire
- sugar from London
- tin from Cornwall
- woollen cloth from Norfolk and Lancashire.

By the 1560s, trade was booming in Europe and gradually England began to share in this prosperity. Merchants in London learnt how to finish their own cloth, and cloth from London began to be exported to the Netherlands and France. Iron, salt, sugar, coal and wool were exported to the markets of Europe. Other ports in England such as Bristol and Liverpool grew quickly as England developed into a centre of trade.

■ Many English towns became prosperous through foreign trade

England's export trade was controlled by a relatively small group of London merchants. These merchants grew rich by buying goods from all over England and then selling them abroad at a higher price to foreign traders. They then began to look further afield for products to sell, and a trade in goods from the New World and from the east developed, as merchant adventurers risked life and limb on the high seas. Men such as Sir Francis Drake sought out new sources of wealth, and at the same time carried the flag of their country to far-off shores.

Joint stock companies

To share the risks, merchants joined together to form what became known as joint stock companies. In this way, both the costs and the revenues from their trading activities were shared, spreading the risk of financial disaster if things went wrong. To finance the ventures, the merchants sold shares in these companies to wealthy landowners, and governments promised such companies a monopoly if they opened up trade with new countries. As a result of the activities of these companies, London's worldwide trading links grew enormously during the sixteenth century, and London became an important commercial centre.

The most important of these new companies, and probably the most famous, was the East India Company. For many years, the Dutch had monopolised the spice trade in the East and in 1599 they more than doubled the price of pepper. Merchants in London were furious and demanded a response. As a result, it was agreed that England would set out to compete with the Dutch and, in 1600, Queen Elizabeth I signed a charter creating the English East India Company.

In 1601, Sir James Lancaster sailed for the East Indies. After two and a half years, and several skirmishes with the Dutch, he returned with a cargo of pepper. The Dutch monopoly had been broken and the East India Company rapidly prospered.

London's growing trade

As London's trade grew, so new facilities were needed to cope with it, and new docks and quays were built for loading and unloading the goods. Elizabeth was keen to earn as much revenue from the growing trade as possible, and in 1588 she set up a commission to nominate those **legal quays** at which foreign goods were to be unloaded. These quickly became overcrowded, and additional ones, called **sufferance wharves**, were nominated. Needless to say, the owners of these quays became extremely rich.

London's place as a leading centre of trade was greatly assisted in 1576 when the port of Antwerp was destroyed by Spanish troops seeking to put down a revolt by Dutch Protestants. Antwerp had been the leading commercial centre in Europe since the early sixteenth century, and English merchants such as Sir Thomas Gresham were quick to seize on the opportunity that this presented.

Write a sentence or two about the following:

(a) London merchants

(b) Joint stock companies

(c) The English East India Company

(d) Antwerp

Exercise 5.3

Write a list of reasons for the growth of England's trade abroad. Write the most important reason at the top and then put other reasons in order of importance below it. In a paragraph explain why you ranked the reasons in this order.

The poor

The first half of the sixteenth century saw a significant increase in the number of poor people in England. The population was rising, prices were rising and unemployment was rising.

There were a number of reasons for the rise in unemployment during this period:

1 The move from arable to sheep farming, and the enclosures that accompanied it, reduced the opportunities for peasant farmers.
2 The Dissolution of the Monasteries meant that thousands of men previously employed in the monasteries were now out of work.
3 The government's insistence that nobles reduced the number of their **retainers under arms** (their private armies) meant that these men were forced to look for other work.

To make matters worse, there was a rise in population from about 2.8 million in 1500, to around 4 million by the end of the century, greatly increasing the pressure on the number of jobs available.

Linked to this, prices increased, probably trebling during the sixteenth century.

There were a number of reasons for the rise in prices, or inflation, over this period:

Population growth

The growing population meant increased demand for necessities such as bread, cheese, meat and ale; but supply of these

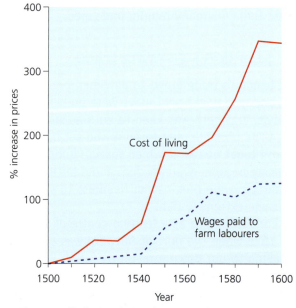

■ The rate of inflation during the sixteenth century

could not keep up. As more people competed to buy the same amount of goods, prices rose.

Debasement of the coinage

In the sixteenth century, coins were made of gold and silver. The silver coin, called a shilling, for example, contained a shilling's worth of silver. People using coins thus had confidence that the value of their money was linked to the value of the precious metal in it. However, Tudor governments realised that they could produce coins with a reduced amount of gold or silver in them, thus allowing them to mint more coins for the same amount of gold or silver metal. For governments trying to finance expensive foreign wars, this was extremely useful. Wolsey was the first to debase the coinage in this way in 1526–27, and governments between 1544–51 made a succession of devaluations that are referred to as 'the Great Debasement'.

Increased government spending

Tudor governments often seemed to be short of money, but this did not stop them spending, especially on foreign wars. As more money was spent, so more money went into circulation, and as the value of this coinage was regularly being debased, prices rose.

Bad harvests

A succession of bad harvests over the period decreased the amount of food available, forcing prices to increase.

Land sales

Following the Dissolution of the Monasteries in the 1530s, the nobility, gentry and merchants scrambled to buy land, forcing up prices.

The effect of all this was to push more and more people into poverty, and to force a growing number of people to leave their homes and to go in search of work in other parishes or towns. The governments of Henry VIII, Edward VI and Mary were not really concerned about the hardship that this caused. What seems to have been their chief concern was the threat to law and order posed by wandering beggars and vagrants, and the various governments took sometimes brutal steps to try to contain this.

By the late sixteenth century, about 10 000 people were making their living by begging or stealing. Children were sometimes deliberately injured by their parents to get sympathy

■ A beggar being whipped; note the grim scene through the archway; woodcut c.1567

from people and thus more chance of help. Gangs of poor people found that stealing was easier than working or begging. Vagabonds took to the streets and the rich lived in fear for their property.

Vagrants or beggars were classed as the 'impotent poor' and, by an Act of Parliament of 1547, anyone unemployed for three days or more was classified as a vagrant. Such people were marked with a 'V' and could be whipped, imprisoned or even killed. Vagrants found outside their own parishes were sent back to where they had come from, but this made matters worse, as they already knew that there was no work for them there.

And of course, after the Dissolution of the Monasteries, any chance these people might have had of receiving food and shelter in a monastery was taken away.

The Elizabethan Poor Laws

To attempt to deal with these problems, Elizabeth's government passed a series of Poor Laws in 1597 and 1601. These laws identified two types of poor people, who were to be treated very differently (see below).

The Poor Laws were successful to a certain extent. They did distinguish between different types of poor people, so that those who were really deserving would be helped. This was the first time that a government and the richer citizens had organised proper help for the poor. The system lasted until the nineteenth century and saved many people from extreme poverty and starvation.

The deserving poor	The idle poor
The deserving poor were either unable to work through illness or disability, or were poor for other reasons such as being widowed.	The idle poor were fit and healthy, but did not work through laziness.
These were seen as deserving of help and charity. Each parish had two **Overseers of the Poor**. They had to collect money from the rich, called the **Poor Rate**, and distribute it to help the deserving poor. If a parish had a poorhouse, the poor would receive **indoor relief** there. If there was no poorhouse, then the poor would receive **outdoor relief** in their own homes. From 1536, parishes were encouraged to raise funds through voluntary contributions to assist the deserving poor.	These were seen as undeserving of charity and a threat to the government. They were whipped and sent back to the parish they had been born in, where they would be made to work. If they carried on begging they would be sent to a **house of correction** or hanged.

However, although the laws did offer some means of help, they did nothing to stop the poor being poor in the first place.

Exercise 5.4

1 **(a)** Make a list of all the different reasons for inflation in the sixteenth century.

   (b) Are there links between any of the reasons? Explain at least one link.

   (c) What do you think was the most important reason for inflation? Explain your answer.

> In comparison with the sixteenth century, how does poor relief work today? Does society now make a distinction between the 'deserving' and 'idle' poor?

2 Write a sentence or two on each of the following:

(a) Overseers

(b) Idle poor

(c) Deserving poor

(d) Indoor relief

(e) Outdoor relief

(f) Poorhouses

3 Imagine that you are a poor man or woman, forced into poverty by unemployment and rising prices. Write an account of what happens to you, being sure to state whether you are to be considered deserving or idle. Bring in as much detail from this section as you can.

Exercise 5.5

1 There are links between the causes of poverty in the sixteenth century. For example, rising prices led to unemployment in the cloth industry. Construct a flow diagram to show further links between the causes.

2 Outline two possible problems with trying to separate the deserving poor from the idle poor.

◯ Towns

Only a small part of the population of Tudor England lived in towns, but towns played a vital role in the economy and were growing fast, as can be seen from these very approximate estimates of population:

	1500	1600
London	60 000	250 000
Bristol	14 000	20 000
Norwich	10 000	20 000
York	10 000	12 000
Exeter	8 000	9 000

Tudor towns were dirty, smelly and crowded. There were no proper sewers or drains; rubbish, manure and human waste would gather in the streets, with no dustmen to carry it away. The rivers were heavily polluted with the foul waters draining away off the streets and disease was rife.

Tradesmen tended to live and work next to each other, with particular parts of a town given over to each trade. The street names

■ An artist's impression of a Tudor town

of any large town today give vital clues to where the various trades were originally located, and this is most obvious in the City of London, the area, one mile square, that represents the original walled city. Here you will find wonderful sounding streets within a short walk of the Tower of London with the following names: Cornmarket Street, Poultry, Bread Street, Limeburner Lane, Hosier Lane, Shoe Lane, Cowcross Street, Leather Lane, Granary Road, Ironmonger Lane, Turnmill Street and Weaver Street, to name just a few.

Water was gathered from pumps or wells, either in the street or, if one was lucky, inside one's own house. The quality of this water was highly questionable and beer was often preferred as a daily drink.

Tudor streets were often narrow, built just wide enough to allow a horse and cart to pass, and usually unpaved. As more and more houses were built with chimneys, so these grew taller. Two- or three-storey houses crowded together, with the upper storeys jutting out over the street below and practically touching the upper storeys of the houses on the other side of the street. Walking these streets at night must have been an unpleasant experience, with no street lighting, the light from the sky above crowded out by the overhanging houses, and no way of seeing what one was stepping in!

Given the filthy condition of the towns, it is not surprising that outbreaks of disease were common and we will see in Chapter 8 what happened when the plague took hold of London's streets.

> Next time you visit your local town, be sure to look at the street names and you are likely to find similar records of who lived and worked there, 500 years ago.

◯ Homes

By the sixteenth century, houses were no longer doubling up as castles. Indeed, kings no longer wished their subjects to be able to defend themselves in the way that they had, and the great houses that sprang up in this period were magnificent palaces rather than formidable fortresses.

Building was seen as a sign of one's status and wealth, and the immense grandeur of Hampton Court, built by Cardinal Wolsey as a home for himself before Henry VIII turned it into a royal palace, or Burghley House, the home of William Cecil, are signs of quite how rich the super rich could become.

Those who could not afford a home on this scale were nevertheless building substantial houses, with timber frames filled in with either wattle-and-daub or bricks; homes such as Little Moreton Hall in Cheshire, for

■ Little Moreton Hall in Cheshire – a moated manor house

example, which survives today as a perfect example of an Elizabethan gentleman's home. Such houses now had at least one chimney, and this greatly increased their stability and allowed for more storeys. Rooves were still usually thatched, although tiles were becoming more widely used.

These homes were more comfortable than the draughty castles or manors of the Middle Ages. They had lattice windows which opened, oak panelling on the walls, and wooden floorboards or black-and-white tiles on the floor. What furniture there was would have been solid and usually made of oak. Huge beds and dressers were passed down from generation to generation, often being the most significant items in people's wills.

The poor, however, had none of these luxuries. They continued to live in simple huts with one or two rooms. They had no chimneys and smoke from their fires escaped through a hole in the thatched roof. Floors were of hard earth and furniture was very basic – benches, stools, a table and perhaps a wooden chest. They slept on the floor or on mattresses stuffed with straw. Those who were more fortunate would lay their mattress on ropes strung across a wooden frame.

Pastimes

During the sixteenth century, dancing was an important way for couples to meet. Music and singing were popular throughout the Tudor period and in rich households the whole family would gather to sing and play on musical instruments such as the lute, **viol**, flute, virginals or **spinet**. This was the age of the composers Byrd, Tallis and Taverner.

Henry VIII was a great sportsman. As well as hunting, sports that were popular at this time included bowls, archery and royal (or real) tennis. Football was also played and we have a number of contemporary references to the game:

Everybody tries to throw his opponent down on the nose, even on stone … necks are broken; sometimes legs; sometimes arms; noses gush out with blood. Everybody is cut and bruised.

As well as these sports that are familiar to us, many people in the sixteenth century liked sports that today seem cruel, such as bear-baiting or cockfighting. In bear-baiting, a bear was chained to a stake to be attacked by specially trained dogs. The spectators would place bets on how long the bear would survive, or how many dogs would be killed. In cockfighting, cockerels would be armed with sharp spurs on their claws and put in a ring to fight. Again, bets were laid as to which bird would win.

The theatre, too, became popular at this time, and it was under Elizabeth that William Shakespeare first began to perform and write plays. We will learn more about this in Chapter 6.

Women

Women in the Tudor age were held to be inferior to men. When a woman married, she gave herself and her property over to her husband, and was expected to show total obedience to her husband in all things. As the Scottish Protestant leader John Knox wrote, 'Woman, in her greatest perfection, was made to serve and obey man.'

The oldest man in a family was legally responsible for what all members of the household did. Only in the most exceptional circumstances could a woman be considered head of a family, which makes it all the more remarkable that this period saw not one but two Queens of England.

A woman's husband could sell off any land or wealth that she had owned before the marriage if he so wished, although this did not extend to her clothes or personal jewellery. As for a wife who committed adultery, she could expect to be severely punished, as Catherine Howard found out, and a nobleman could have his adulterous wife burnt at the stake if the king or queen agreed.

Girls' education

Girls rarely received any type of formal education, but were instead prepared for their adult role as wife and mother. They were taught various skills and crafts, depending on their social position.

Girls from a poor home were taught practical skills such as cooking, cleaning, washing, making clothes and, in an age before refrigeration, how to preserve food. These tasks demanded great skill and would keep a girl occupied from dawn until dusk. Girls from the homes of the

> The Tudor view of a woman's rights seems harsh but a very similar attitude prevailed until fairly recently. When were women finally regarded as equal partners, able to hold property in their own right, rather than in their husbands' names?

rich were more likely to receive education in science and the arts, but would also learn how to manage a household, do fancy needlework and prepare meals. It was generally believed that teaching girls to read and write was less important than teaching them more practical skills; and although Queen Mary and Queen Elizabeth were both well schooled in Latin and French, two of Henry VIII's wives – Jane Seymour and Catherine Howard – could barely read at all.

Marriage and childbearing

Young ladies from rich families had very little choice over who their husband would be. Marriages were frequently arranged to bring two families more closely together, or to increase the landholding of the husband's family, and for this reason it would not have been uncommon for a couple not to have met until the day of their wedding. A woman brought a **dowry** (an amount of money or property) with her when she married as a contribution to the new family household: this might be anything from a few sheep to vast lands and huge amounts of money.

There was no legal minimum age for marriage and many girls married as young as fourteen. The poor tended to marry off their daughters as soon as they could, on the grounds that if girls did not marry they would remain a burden to their family, an extra mouth to feed and not bringing in any income.

Tudor ladies did not have reliable methods of contraception, and it was not unusual for wives to be pregnant every twelve months for several years. Pregnancy was dangerous, and death in childbirth, either for the mother or the child, was not at all unusual. Indeed it was common at this time for a pregnant wife, while preparing a new baby's nursery, to be also making arrangements for the baby should she, the mother, die in childbirth.

The actual act of childbirth was assisted by a midwife. There were no maternity hospitals and for most families, the midwife was simply an elderly female relative or neighbour, someone who had had children of her own and knew what to expect. Only rich families could afford to have a doctor on hand for a birth. Even if the delivery of a baby was successful, the mother could still fall prey to illness due to the lack of hygiene during childbirth. The most famous Tudor casualty of this was Jane Seymour, who died shortly after giving birth to Edward VI. Puerperal (or childbed) fever and post-birth infections were both killers.

How did women spend their time?

If we are to believe the account of a visitor to England in 1575, rich women enjoyed pleasant and carefree lives:

They spend time walking, riding, playing cards and visiting friends, talking to neighbours and making merry with them. England is called the paradise of married women.

Certainly, the wife of a rich husband had servants to do the housework. But it wasn't all leisure as the description above suggests. A woman had to keep an eye on her servants and make sure that they did their job properly. Everything had to be right for when her husband returned to the house.

So, how hard a woman worked depended on the money her husband had. For the poor, it was rather different. Poor women cared for the children and cooked the meals, but they also had to work in the fields with their husbands, spin wool and mend the family's clothes.

Women's clothes

As we might expect, women in Tudor times dressed in a way that reflected the fashion of the day, but also the amount of money they had available to spend on clothes. Dresses tended to be modest, reaching to the ground and with long sleeves, and sometimes with high ruffs at the neck as worn by men. They were made of heavy fabric and were probably quite uncomfortable. Hair was usually worn up, especially by married women, and it was quite unusual to see a woman with her hair hanging loose.

For queens and noble ladies, ceremonial dresses would have been colourful, often encrusted with jewels, and extremely expensive.

■ Poor women helping at harvest; from a book of hours c.1520–30

Exercise 5.6

1 Make a copy of the following table and then complete the sections using evidence from this chapter and your knowledge of the position of women today.

	Women in the sixteenth century	Women today
Marriage		
Education		
Childbirth		
Legal rights		
Employment		

2 Explain what you think is the greatest difference between the position of women then and now.

Exercise 5.7

SOURCE A: An extract from Anthony Fitzherbert's *Book of Husbandry*, written in 1522.

It is a wife's occupation to winnow* corn, to make hay and shear corn. In time of need she should help her husband fill the muck wagon, drive the plough, load hay, go to market to sell butter, cheese, milk, eggs, chickens, pigs, geese and corn.

* winnow – to shake out corn to separate the grain from the rest of the plant

SOURCE B: An extract from Thomas Platter's *Travels in England*, written in 1599.

The women of England are fair and pretty. They have more freedom than in any other countries and know just how to make good use of it. They often stroll around or drive out by coach in beautiful clothes and then men have to put up with such behaviour and may not punish them for it. Indeed the good wives often beat their men.

SOURCE C: A woman playing the clavichord, a sixteenth-century painting attributed to Jan Sanders van Hemessen.

1 What can you learn from Source A about a woman's position in the home?

2 What does Source B suggest about the lifestyle of women?

3 Does Source C support the evidence of Source A about the lifestyle of women in the sixteenth century? Explain your answer.

4 Which of the sources do you think gives the most accurate impression of women in the sixteenth century? Explain your answer using evidence from this section on women.

5 Using all the sources and your own knowledge, how far do you agree that sixteenth-century women were treated as equal to men?

6 James I and Charles I

James I, 1603–25

Elizabeth remained unmarried and childless throughout her reign, but there was little doubt as to who would succeed her when she died. Her cousin, Mary Queen of Scots, had considered herself a better claimant to the English throne than Elizabeth herself, and on Elizabeth's death, Mary's son, King James VI of Scotland, was proclaimed King James I of England.

Like so many monarchs of this period, James had had a turbulent childhood. His mother had fled from Scotland not long after his birth, accused of murdering his father, Henry, Lord Darnley. He had been proclaimed King of Scotland as a mere babe in arms, but faced a lonely childhood, troubled by what probably felt like physical abuse from his teachers, political abuse from his nobles and religious abuse from his clergy. He was well educated, however, and like Henry VIII before him, was interested in Biblical studies, although he did earn the rather unflattering nickname, 'the wisest fool in Christendom'.

James, unlike his mother Mary Queen of Scots, was a Protestant. Elizabeth's long reign had seen a number of failed Catholic attempts to challenge her position and the succession of a Protestant king looked sure to remove, once and for all, the threat of a return to the religion of Rome. The increasingly outspoken Puritans in England hoped that James, educated in the ways of Calvin, would be sympathetic to their demands for a more pure form of religion. So when James entered London, after a long and tiring ride from Edinburgh, he was mobbed and cheered by the people.

■ James I; from a portrait produced in 1618 by Paul van Somer

Problems facing James

James faced two main problems when he came to the throne, which we should be familiar with by now: religion and finances.

Religion

The Reformation which had spread from Europe to England during the sixteenth century had been embraced in Scotland when John Knox, a Scottish Protestant who had studied in Geneva with Calvin, returned to Scotland and persuaded the Scottish Reformation Parliament of 1560 to lead Scotland from moderate Lutheranism to a more radical Calvinism. He and his supporters became known as **Presbyterians**.

When James arrived in England in 1603, many Puritans hoped that he would introduce these more radical forms of Protestantism to England. They presented him with a petition signed by a thousand clerics, the Millenary Petition, calling for alterations to the Elizabethan Prayer Book and the abolition of bishops.

James agreed to listen to the Puritans, but was also keen to appease the Catholic sympathisers. One of his first acts was to abolish **recusancy fines**, levied on Catholics who refused to attend Protestant church services. He also gave important posts to two prominent Catholics, the Earls of Northumberland and Northampton.

However, despite his moves to appease them, James faced two Catholic plots in 1603, the Main Plot and the Bye Plot, and this caused him to reconsider his leniency towards them, which had been extremely unpopular with Anglicans.

In January 1604, a Church conference was held at Hampton Court. At the conference, James continued the policy Elizabeth had followed of appealing to as wide a body of the Church as he could. But if the Puritans thought that James was going to give in to all their demands, they were disappointed. When asked to approve the removal of bishops from the Church of England, James is famously reported to have shouted, 'No bishop, no king.' Some Puritans, realising that they stood little hope of seeing their demands accepted, decided to leave England and sailed to America to start a new life in the New World. The most famous of these were the Pilgrim Fathers who sailed in the *Mayflower* in September 1620. As for the Catholics, James was openly hostile to them and shortly afterwards reversed his decision on recusancy fines, which was to lead to the Gunpowder Plot (see page 83).

One positive thing that did come out of the Hampton Court Conference was James's commissioning of another translation of the Bible into English. This translation became known as the *Authorised Version* and is still used in some churches today. It is now commonly described as the *King James Version*.

> The voyage of the *Mayflower* is of great importance to Americans. Find out all you can about the Founding Fathers and the journey of the ship from Plymouth.

Money and Parliament

As king, James was always in need of money. As his reign progressed, the methods he used to raise finance brought him increasingly into conflict with Parliament. Elizabeth's war with Spain and the conflict in Ireland had left the royal exchequer empty. James was able to bring peace with both countries, but he was an extravagant monarch and his court reflected his lavish approach to life. Sir Anthony Weldon, a bitter critic of the Stuarts who died in 1648, wrote of James:

He was very liberal of what he had not in his own grip, and would rather part with 100 pounds he never had in his keeping than one twenty shilling piece within his own custody; he spent much, and had much use of his subjects' purses, which bred some clashings with them in Parliament.

As a result, James needed money, and to get money, he had to turn to Parliament.

While Elizabeth had expressed impatience at the idea that her parliaments should question her actions or challenge her authority, James went further. James was a firm believer in the **Divine Right of Kings**. This stated that kings derive their right to rule directly from God and were not therefore accountable to their subjects. In 1603 James expressed his views on monarchy as follows:

It is not lawful to argue with the king's power. It is contempt in a subject to say that a king cannot do this or that. Kings are the makers of laws and as the king is overlord of the whole land so he has power of life and death over every person that lives in the same.

In 1604, in a speech to his first Parliament, he went even further:

The state of monarchy is the supremest thing on Earth: for kings are not only God's assistants upon Earth, but even by God himself they are called gods in the Scriptures. As to dispute what God may do is blasphemy, so is it treason in subjects to dispute what a king may do. I will not have my power disputed, but I shall be willing to rule according to my laws.

The Gunpowder Plot

Remember, remember the fifth of November

Gunpowder, treason and plot.

I see no reason why gunpowder, treason

Should ever be forgot …

Following the Hampton Court Conference, it was clear to most Catholics that the only way that they could achieve religious toleration was to remove James from the throne. Accordingly, a daring plot was hatched to blow him up as he opened a new session of Parliament. The date fixed for the opening of the new session was 5 November 1605.

CONCILIVM SEPTEM NOBILIVM ANGLORVM CONIVRANTIVM IN NECEM IACOBI·I·
MAGNÆ·BRITANNIÆ·REGIS·TOTIVSQ·ANGLICI·CONVOCATI·PARLEMENTI·

Bates · Robert Winter · Christopher Wright · Iohn Wright · Thomas Percy · Guido Fawkes · Robert Catesby · Thomas Winter

■ The Gunpowder Plotters; a contemporary engraving believed to be by the Dutch artist Crispijn van de Passe the Elder

The Gunpowder Plot was devised in May 1604 by Robert Catesby and Thomas Percy. At first, the conspirators planned to tunnel underneath the House of Commons, but the need for this was removed when they conveniently managed to rent a cellar under the building. Large amounts of gunpowder were brought into the cellar and the idea was that this would be ignited as the King was in the House above. However, one of the plotters, Francis Tresham, feared that his brother-in-law Lord Monteagle might be killed in the resulting explosion. On 26 October 1605, Tresham sent an anonymous letter warning Monteagle not to attend the opening of Parliament because 'a great calamity would consume it':

My Lord, out of the love I bear to some of your friends, I have a care for your preservation. Therefore I would advise you, as you tender your life, to devise some excuse to shift of your attendance at this Parliament, for God and man hath concurred to punish the wickedness of this time. And think not slightly of this advertisement but retire yourself into your country, where you may expect the event in safety, for though there be no appearance of any stir, yet I say they shall receive a terrible blow, the Parliament, and yet they shall not see who hurts them.

Monteagle, realising the significance of the letter, at once gave it to Robert Cecil, James's Chief Minister.

On the night of 4 November 1605, the day before Parliament was scheduled to open, one of the conspirators, Guy Fawkes, was arrested in the cellar beneath the Parliament buildings. He was brought before the King and, over the next few days, was tortured until gradually he revealed details of the plot and the names of his fellow conspirators. James moved fast. By 7 November, almost all of the conspirators had been captured. They were tried and in early 1606 were hanged, drawn and quartered.

After the plot, James gave Lord Monteagle a pension of £500 for life, plus lands worth a further £200 per year.

Some people believe that the case against Guy Fawkes was fabricated by the government, and that it was an elaborate way of making people hate Catholics. The historian R. Crampton argued in 1990 that there was no evidence of a tunnel having been dug or of any gunpowder having been found, and no proof that the letter sent to Lord Monteagle was written by Francis Tresham:

If Guy Fawkes's case came up before the Court of Appeal today, the judges would surely acquit him.

But whatever the truth, Catholics were viewed with great suspicion after 1605.

Shakespeare and the Globe Theatre

James I enjoyed lavish feasts and parties, and a form of entertainment that was becoming very popular at this time – the theatre. This was the age of great writers such as Edmund Spenser and Christopher Marlowe, but by far the most famous was William Shakespeare.

Shakespeare was born in 1564 and, having spent his early years in Stratford-upon-Avon, moved to London, and worked as an actor and writer of plays, of which 38 have survived. He was popular at Court, and his group of actors was called the King's Men. They built their own theatre, the Globe, which was open to the sky but had covered areas over the stage and where the people who could afford to sat. The poor would stand in an open area in front of the stage and were called 'groundlings'.

Shakespeare wrote three types of play: history plays, tragedies and comedies. Everyone from king to groundlings enjoyed the bawdy humour of the comedies, the fast-moving action of the history plays and the intense drama of the tragedies. But although they were written for entertainment, many of them had a political message which would have appealed to the King.

> Guy Fawkes has been described as a 'Catholic terrorist'. Do you agree with this view? How does the Gunpowder Plot compare with modern acts, or attempted acts, of terrorism?

■ The arrest of Guy Fawkes

■ The interior of the Swan Theatre in Southwark; from a drawing produced in 1596 by Johannes de Wit

Exercise 6.1

1 Write an article for a newspaper, dated 6 November 1605, about the Gunpowder Plot. Use the following title:

CATHOLIC PLOT DISCOVERED

2 Explain what the consequences of the Gunpowder Plot were for James I.

3 Read the extract below, taken from a letter written by an Italian Catholic visitor to England after the plot in 1605. How useful is this source in helping you understand the treatment of the Gunpowder Plotters?

> *Some claim that there was foul play, and that the government secretly spun a web to trap these poor gentlemen.*

Exercise 6.2

1 Use the internet or your library to find out what you can about one of Shakespeare's plays, and then write a set of programme notes for a performance of the play.

2 In Shakespeare's play *Richard III*, Richard is portrayed as an evil man. Look back to the beginning of this book and re-read the section on Henry VII. Can you suggest reasons why Richard was portrayed in this unflattering way?

◯ Trouble with Parliament

In 1604 James asked Parliament to ratify a full union of the Scottish and English Crowns, and to grant him a subsidy to pay for the expensive war with Spain, which had dragged on since the Spanish Armada. When it refused, he **prorogued** Parliament – it was discontinued without the session being formally ended. James's relations with Parliament had got off to a bad start.

As he was still short of money, James turned to such measures as selling peerages, knighthoods and **monopolies** (which gave a company the exclusive right to sell a product). This raised money for the Crown, but was unpopular with Parliament, which claimed that it was illegal. James suggested that Parliament should grant him an income of £200 000 per annum, but that too was rejected.

In 1614, James called a second Parliament, the so-called Addled Parliament, but dissolved

■ George Villiers, Duke of Buckingham; a seventeenth-century portrait

it after only eight weeks when again it failed to do what he wanted with regard to the raising of taxation.

By now, James had become reliant on the advice of his 'favourite', George Villiers, who was later to become the Duke of Buckingham. James called Buckingham his 'sweetheart', and said of him:

You may be sure that I love the Duke of Buckingham more than anyone else, and more than you who are here assembled.

Buckingham became extremely powerful through his friendship with the King, and thus unpopular. He involved himself in making policy decisions, and Parliament resented this. He also made himself rich by selling offices and monopolies, and, in 1621, when James called his third Parliament, MPs launched an investigation into Buckingham's abuses. This Parliament was short lived, however, because it made the mistake of trying to discuss foreign policy and the proposed marriage of James's son Charles to the Spanish *Infanta* (the daughter of the Spanish King). Like Elizabeth before him, James disputed the right of the House of Commons to discuss whatever they wished and the Parliament was dissolved.

Buckingham favoured the royal marriage and that year accompanied Charles on an unofficial visit to Spain. The visit was a disaster and there was great relief in England that the marriage to a Roman Catholic would not take place. Buckingham was humiliated and returned to England now advocating war with Spain, which gained him the support of Parliament, but James was angry with his favourite.

The final Parliament of James's reign was in 1624. James's financial troubles were by then severe, and he was now relying on the efforts of his Lord Treasurer, Sir Lionel Cranfield, to restore his finances. Parliament disapproved of Cranfield, and **impeached** him (removed him from office). Furthermore, as if deliberately to anger James, Parliament granted a subsidy for the renewed war against Spain which Buckingham had proposed and which James opposed.

King James I died on 27 March 1625. He had had mixed fortunes as King of England, but at least he was able to pass on his crown securely to his son Charles.

Exercise 6.3

SOURCE A: from Francis Osborne, *Traditionall Memoyres on the Raigne of King James the First*, 1658:

The manner [of his feasts] was to have the board covered, at the first entrance of the guests, with dishes, as high as a tall man could well reach, filled with the choicest and dearest viands sea or land could afford: and all this once seen, and having feasted the eyes of the invited, was in a manner thrown away, and fresh set on to the same height, having only this advantage of the other, that it was hot … And after such suppers huge banquets no less profuse, a waiter returning his servant home with a cloak-bag full of dried sweet-meats, and confects, valued to his lordship at more than ten shillings the pound. I am cloyd with the repetition of this excess, no less than scandalized at the continuance of it.

1   What do we learn about the extravagance at James's court from Source A?

2   Re-read Sir Anthony Weldon's description of James on page 83. Does this agree or disagree with the account in Source A?

3   Which source do you find more useful in helping us to understand why James ran into money difficulties during his reign?

4   Using both the sources and your own knowledge, explain why James was in trouble with Parliament throughout his reign.

Exercise 6.4

1   (a) What were the problems facing James when he became king? Draw a flow diagram to show how the problems are connected.

   (b) Rank the problems in order of importance. Write an essay explaining carefully how you arrived at your decision about the most important problem.

Charles I, 1625–49

Charles I was born in 1600, the second son of James I and Anne of Denmark. He was a shy and artistic youth, only 5 feet 3 inches (1m 60cm) tall, and suffered from a stammer. His elder brother Henry died in 1612, leaving him as heir to the throne.

   As he grew up he became friendly with James's favourite, the Duke of Buckingham, and perhaps under his influence Charles, who was deeply religious, became interested in the rituals of the High Anglicans. This was a group within the Church which, while not Catholic, nonetheless favoured ceremony and lavish ornamentation in their services, and – in contrast to the Puritans and Presbyterians – placed a high degree of importance on the role of bishops and priests.

■ Charles I; a portrait painted in the seventeenth century by Daniel Mytens

While Charles's religious views were unpopular with the Puritans in England and the Presbyterians in Scotland, so his views on monarchy brought him into conflict with the growing middle classes, who had made their money through trade. Charles, like his father, believed passionately in the Divine Right of Kings, and was utterly convinced that his power came from God. With such a view of his own importance, this made him most unpopular with MPs and those who were rising in wealth through their own efforts, rather than through the family ties of aristocracy and royalty.

Early problems

Charles inherited a royal treasury that had been drained by his extravagant father. While the royal household had cost around £9500 to run under Elizabeth, this figure had risen to £35 000 under James, and things did not improve under Charles. Charles was a generous patron of the arts, lavishing money on painters such as Titian, Raphael and Van Dyck, and on musicians who entertained his court. None of this made him popular with those outside his immediate circle.

Charles, like his father before him, was heavily influenced by the unpopular Duke of Buckingham. Buckingham had led a disastrous campaign against the Spanish at Cadiz, and was planning to attack the French too. His management of these campaigns was poor, the expense was crippling, and Charles had to intervene in Parliament to prevent his friend from being impeached. Eventually, in 1628, Buckingham was stabbed to death by a naval officer, John Felton, so that problem, at least, went away.

In the matter of religion, too, he became unpopular, and Parliament was most alarmed when Charles married the Catholic sister of the King of France, Henrietta Maria. With his leanings towards High Anglicanism, and its religious forms, this seemed to push him away from the radical Protestantism of the Puritans and back towards the Roman Catholicism that his predecessors had stamped out. Charles's marriage to a Roman Catholic made people alarmed about how far he might go.

Problems with money

In 1627, Charles asked Parliament for money, but the members gave him just one-tenth of what he needed. Parliament was dismissed and, in desperation, Charles had no choice but to extract forced loans from his subjects:

Our treasures exhausted and our coffers empty, we summoned a Parliament, but not finding that success therein which we had just hope to expect, we are resolved to require the aid of our good and loving subjects by lending us a sufficient sum of money to be repaid them as soon as we shall be in any way able to do so.

When in 1628 Charles tried to increase the duty on wine and other goods, a group of MPs led by John Pym drew up a **Petition of Right** which stated:

> *It is declared and enacted by a statute made in the time of the reign of King Edward I ... that no tax shall be laid or levied by the king or his heirs in this realm, without the goodwill and assent of [Parliament] ... Yet nevertheless lately your people have been required to lend certain sums of money to your Majesty, and many of them, upon their refusal to do so, have been imprisoned ... against the laws and free custom of the realm.*

Charles initially agreed to the demand that he stop taking forced loans, and imprisoning people without a trial. In 1629, however, Parliament presented Charles with the 'Three Resolutions' and the King thought that his authority was being challenged. Furiously, Charles dismissed Parliament and for the next eleven years, until 1640, he ruled without it. Charles called this a period of 'personal rule', but his enemies knew it as the 'Eleven Year Tyranny'.

Charles now found that, if he were to rule without Parliament, he needed to cut his costs and find alternative sources of revenue. With the warmongering, but inept, Buckingham dead, Charles made peace with France and Spain. He then used various methods to raise extra money:

Legal fines
The king had the right to collect fines from law courts. Charles revived old laws that had fallen into disuse – and then fined people for breaking them.

Sale of monopolies and knighthoods
Charles raised money from rich merchants by selling them monopolies, the exclusive right to trade in a particular area, and by selling knighthoods.

Ship money
In the past, only counties bordering the sea had been expected to bear the cost of taxes for building ships, but in 1635, Charles extended the tax to the whole country.

These measures brought Charles into conflict with men such as John Hampden, a rich country gentleman and an MP. He refused to pay his **ship money**, on the grounds that the king had no right to collect it. His lawyer said:

> *The king should take nothing from his subjects except with the agreement of Parliament.*

Hampden was tried in court, and it was decided as follows:

The king should have the right to demand, and the people must pay, money for the defence of the kingdom.

Hampden had to pay up, but in the years ahead he remained a bitter opponent of the King.

Exercise 6.5

1 Write a sentence on each of the following:

   (a) Forced loans

   (b) Fines

   (c) Monopolies

   (d) Ship money

2 Write a reply from Charles to the Petition of Right defending his methods of raising money.

3

> **SOURCE A:** An extract from *A History of the Great Rebellion*, written in the 1660s by the Earl of Clarendon. Clarendon was a close advisor to Charles I's son for several years and is writing about the eleven years' rule without Parliament.
>
> *In this time the kingdom enjoyed the greatest calm and the fullest measure of happiness that any people in any age for so long a time have been blessed with. England was secure. The country was rich and was enjoying the pleasure of its own wealth. The Protestant religion was advanced against Rome by the writings of Archbishop Laud more than it had since the Reformation.*

   (a) What can you learn from Source A about Charles's eleven years of personal rule?

   (b) How useful is Source A as evidence of Charles's years of personal rule?

Problems with religion

Charles's problems with money may have been severe, but it was religion that provided the spark for civil war. For many years, the Puritans in England had been growing in importance and as Charles brought pressure to bear on Parliament to listen to his demands for money, so the Puritans brought pressure to bear on Charles to listen to their demands for a purer form of religion.

The Puritans

Puritans were extreme Protestants, the natural successors to Calvin, who believed that man had a relationship with God which was personal, and did not rely on the intervention of priests or bishops. Puritans hated any form of ceremony or ornament, which they claimed only acted as a distraction. They distrusted bishops and questioned the need for their existence; and they wanted a new Prayer Book that would put their view of Christianity at the heart of the established Church.

The Puritans believed that God had chosen them in the fight against sin. They preached sermons and printed pamphlets to spread their ideas, raising fears of public order. But Charles had other views. He believed that he had been chosen by God, and that his authority was not to be challenged by anyone. When the Puritans challenged Charles in Parliament over the role of bishops, he threatened to 'harry them out of the land'.

Archbishop Laud and the 'Laudian Church'

In 1633, Charles appointed William Laud as Archbishop of Canterbury. Laud was determined to bring total uniformity to the Church. He was a Protestant, but distrusted the Puritans, thinking that they had far too much influence. However, rather than steering a middle road through the various factions, Laud set out to make church services more elaborate, saying:

> *Nothing can be correct without some ceremonies, and in religion the more old-fashioned they are the better.*

Laud made priests wear vestments once more, and reintroduced stained-glass windows into churches. He also felt that bishops were vital in the Church as local leaders and authority figures. Laud's love of ceremony and symbolism – what he called the 'beauty of holiness' – was shared by King Charles, but it was loathed by Puritans, who regarded Laud's ideas as unholy.

The Puritans thought that Laud was turning the Church of England back into the Roman Catholic Church. His persecution of Puritan preachers and pamphleteers made them suspicious of him. This is how some Members of Parliament reacted to Laud's changes:

> *Like a traitor he has tried to ruin true religion and replaced it with Catholic ideas. He has brought in Catholic ceremonies without any agreement and he has cruelly persecuted those who have opposed him.*

Laud's attempts to force uniformity of worship on every parish in England were strongly opposed. In 1637, three religious radicals, William Prynne, Henry Burton and John Bastwick, were imprisoned and tortured – their ears were cut off – for speaking against Laud's policy. The popular rabble-rouser 'Freeborn John' Lilburne was arrested for distributing unlicensed pamphlets in 1638. Anger towards Laud grew and a popular pun developed:

> *Give praise to God, and little Laud* to the devil.*

* Laud is another word for praise (from the Latin *laudo* = I praise).

Scotland and the First Bishops' War

In 1637, Charles and Laud tried to make the Scottish Presbyterians accept a new Prayer Book and to endow Scottish bishops with English-style powers. However, the Scots thought that the Prayer Book was too Catholic in its style, and riots broke out when it was introduced. In St Giles's Cathedral, Edinburgh, the Dean was pelted with sticks and stones, and a woman called Jenny Geddes is supposed to have thrown her prayer stool at his head.

In 1638 the Scottish people signed a **covenant**, or promise, stating:

We promise and declare that we shall with all our means and our lives defend our true Protestant religion, our freedoms and the laws of our kingdoms. We will oppose all the new errors and corruptions.

■ The Arch Prelate of St Andrews, Edinburgh, reading the new service book; from an engraving produced around 1637

Charles refused to give way to the opposition in Scotland. He sent instructions to his general in Scotland as follows:

Say what you need to these rebels. Your aim now must be to win time so that the crowds cause no damage until I attack them. I will die rather than yield to these impertinent and awful demands.

In 1639, Charles sent an army to Scotland to make the Scots accept the new Prayer Book. But to everybody's shock, the English were easily defeated. This short struggle became known as the First Bishops' War.

The following year, Parliament accused Archbishop Laud of treason, resulting in his imprisonment in the Tower of London. Legal delays meant he was not tried until 1644, by which time Charles was in the midst of a civil war and forced to abandon his unpopular Archbishop to his fate. Laud was beheaded on Tower Hill in January 1645.

1 Explain how Charles's religious views brought him into conflict.

2 Explain how Laud's actions led to his being beheaded in 1645.

The Short Parliament and Second Bishops' War

Charles was determined to take revenge on the Scots for his humiliating defeat, but he had no funds to pay for a bigger army. Thomas Wentworth, the Earl of Strafford, advised Charles to call a Parliament and ask for the money. When the MPs refused Charles's request the Parliament was dissolved after only three weeks, during April and May 1640. This was known as the Short Parliament.

Strafford then persuaded Charles to invade Scotland anyway, which began the Second Bishops' War. This again ended in a Scottish victory and Charles was forced to sign the Treaty of Ripon in October 1640, under which he agreed to hand over Newcastle, Northumberland and County Durham to the Scots, and to pay the Scots £850 a day – a huge sum – to pay for the maintenance of a Scottish army there.

The Long Parliament, 1640

Once again, Charles found himself forced to turn to Parliament to ask for money.

The Long Parliament, so called because it was not finally dissolved until 1660, presented a list of grievances to the King. MPs such as John Pym, who had been so vocal in the presentation of the Petition of Right, summarised the complaints against the King:

Firstly, Parliament was dissolved before our complaints were heard. Several gentlemen were imprisoned for speaking freely to Parliament. Secondly, there have been changes in matters of religion. The introduction of Catholic ceremonies and altars, bowing towards the east, pictures, crucifixes, crosses and the like. Thirdly, there is an attack on our property. The taking of taxes, without any grant or law.

In March 1641, Pym then turned his attention to Charles's minister, the Earl of Strafford, who was put on trial for treason. When Strafford was found not guilty, Parliament passed a **Bill of Attainder**, meaning that he could be executed anyway. Charles could not risk another major disagreement with Parliament, so reluctantly he allowed Strafford to be executed in May 1641. Charles was encouraged in this by his wife, Queen Henrietta Maria, who was terrified of the mob gathering in Whitehall. But the King regretted his actions to his dying day, believing that his fate was God's punishment for the betrayal of Strafford.

Forced into a corner, Charles agreed to a series of demands, including:

- the punishment of ministers that Parliament disliked, especially Strafford
- the abolition of ship money and monopolies
- the right of Parliament to choose the king's ministers
- the right of Parliament to be called at least every three years
- the right of MPs to vote against the king's wish to end Parliament
- the abolition of the king's special law courts, such as the Star Chamber, which sat without juries.

Exercise 6.7

1 Add the correct dates to the following events of 1639–41, and then put them in chronological order:

(a) The trial of Strafford

(b) Short Parliament

(c) Second Bishops' War

(d) Long Parliament

(e) First Bishops' War

2 What can you learn about Parliament's grievances against the King from Pym's speech on page 94?

3 Look back at all the reasons for conflict between Charles and Parliament. Make a copy of the table below and complete the boxes. Then answer the questions below.

Political reasons	Economic reasons	Religious reasons

Explain why the differences between Charles I and Parliament led to civil war.

The road to civil war

Charles now found himself on a road that was to lead, eventually, to civil war. Parliament knew that he was growing powerless to act without their agreement, and the main reason for this was financial: without Parliament, Charles had no money.

Trouble in Ireland

In October 1641, there was a rebellion in Ireland. The Catholics in Ireland believed that the English Parliament's anti-Catholic laws were targeted towards them. A force led by Phelim O'Neill rose up in revolt and killed 12 000 Protestants in Ulster. Charles was powerless to put down this rebellion without an army, and he could not raise an army without more money. Pym agreed to provide money for the army, but on condition that Parliament should appoint its commander. 'By God, not for an hour', replied the angry King. But such was the force of Pym's approach that some of his more moderate supporters went back to supporting Charles.

The Grand Remonstrance

In November 1641, Pym submitted to Parliament another list of Charles's mistakes, called the Grand Remonstrance. Chief among Pym's complaints was the influence of the King's ministers, and he proposed that they should in future be appointed by Parliament:

We will not allow a few people around the King, or even the King himself on his own, to decide what the law will be, especially as the King has always relied on a few individuals to help him.

The Remonstrance was approved by Parliament. Charles, who considered himself chosen by God to rule over his people, was furious, and complained:

All the troubles are caused by a handful of evil and ambitious people who want to change the government and Church and to put everyone under their own lawless power.

Charles now decided to show Parliament who was in charge. Urged on by his wife, on 4 January 1642 he went to Westminster with 400 soldiers to arrest five of the most troublesome MPs: John Pym, John Hampden, Arthur Haselrig, Denzil Holles and William Strode. The charge was high treason.

An MP, Sir Ralph Verney, witnessed the event and described what happened. This is part of his account:

The five gentlemen which were to be accused came into the House, and there was information that they should be taken by force. Upon this, the House sent to the Lord Mayor, aldermen, and common council to let them know how the privileges were likely to be broken and the city put into danger, and advised them to look to their security ... A little after, the King came with all his guard ... and two or three hundred soldiers and gentlemen ... He told us he would not break our privileges, but treason had no privilege; he came for those five gentlemen ... He asked the Speaker if they were here, or where they were. The Speaker fell on his knees and said he had neither eyes nor tongue to see or say anything but what they [the MPs] commanded him. Then the King told him that he thought his own eyes were as good as his, and then said his birds were flown.

■ The flight of the five MPs

Many people were shocked at the King's actions. Legally, MPs could not be arrested when they were in the House of Commons. As riots broke out in London, Charles left the capital and went to Hampton Court, not returning until after the Civil War.

The tension between Charles and Parliament worsened over the following months. In February 1642, Puritan MPs again demanded that Charles get rid of bishops, and others even asked for the abolition of the Church of England. MPs who had supported Pym in his challenge of the King now became alarmed at the prospect of the Puritans taking over the country and its religion.

'Parliamentary privilege' is a set of rules that allow MPs to carry out their duties unhindered. What privileges do MPs have today? Are they immune from arrest in the House of Commons?

The Nineteen Propositions

The final trigger for the Civil War came in June 1642 when Parliament passed a set of demands known as the Nineteen Propositions. The most important of these stated that:

- all affairs of state must be agreed with Parliament
- all ministers must be approved by Parliament
- laws against Catholics must be enforced
- parliament must control the army
- the Church must be reformed as Parliament wishes.

The last of these demands caused particular concern to moderate Protestants, who saw it as an attempt by the Puritans to push through religious change contrary to the wishes of the majority of the people. Parliament became divided, with some MPs openly throwing their support behind the King.

Officially, Parliament now had control of the army, but in August 1642 Charles rode to Nottingham and raised his standard, calling on all loyal subjects to join him in his fight against the rebels. The English Civil War had begun.

■ Charles I's force raises the standard at Nottingham

Exercise 6.8

1 **(a)** The Civil War was the result of a conflict between the King and Parliament. Divide a page into two columns. On the left-hand side summarise the beliefs and actions of Charles I that led to the Civil War. On the right-hand side, summarise the beliefs and actions of Members of Parliament.

(b) Now divide a page into three columns. In the first column write the long-term causes of the Civil War. In the second column write the short-term causes (1639–41) and in the third column the final trigger.

2 Explain why both James I and Charles I quarrelled with Parliament in the years 1603–42.

3 Explain who caused greater problems for Charles I: the Puritans or the Catholics?

Exercise 6.9

Read the sources and then answer the question below.

SOURCE A: An extract from the Grand Remonstrance of 1641:

The Court of Star Chamber hath abounded in extravagant censures, not only for the maintenance and improvement of monopolies and their unlawful taxes, but for diverse other causes where there hath been no offence, or very small; whereby His Majesty's subjects have been oppressed by grievous fines, imprisonments, stigmatisings, mutilations, whippings, pillories, gags, confinements, banishments ...

SOURCE B: From an article by historian Graham Seel:

Charles adapted quickly and impressively to changed political circumstances after the meeting of the Long Parliament. During the course of 1641 he assented to bills obliging him to call Parliament at least once every three years, preventing him from dissolving Parliament unless MPs agreed and abolishing the prerogative courts (High Commission and Star Chamber) which had sustained his Personal Rule during the 1630s ... These and other measures won the King support. At least two-fifths of the House of Commons and the vast majority of the House of Lords chose in 1642 to side with Charles and not Parliament.

SOURCE C: Charles I demanding the arrest of the five MPs, 4 January 1642; from a painting produced in 1866 by Charles Cope.

1 Read Source A. Which part of Charles I's government is this extract of the Grand Remonstrance complaining about?

2 In Source B, what point is the historian trying to make about Charles I as a leader?

3 How useful is Source C to a historian studying the causes of the English Civil War? Remember to consider the form and provenance of the source.

4 Using all the sources as evidence and your own knowledge, how far do you think the outbreak of the Civil War was the fault of Charles I?

■ Charles I in Parliament; from a nineteenth-century fresco in the House of Commons, by Charles Cope

7 Civil War and the republican experiment

The Civil War, 1642–49

The Civil War lasted for seven years, during which time families were split, with father fighting against son, and brother against brother. To generalise, though, the two sides were broadly divided as follows:

Royalists	Parliamentarians
● Old nobility	● Lesser gentry
● Courtiers	● Merchants
● Roman Catholics and Anglicans	● Puritans and Presbyterians
● Countrymen	● Townsmen

The Royalists were known as Cavaliers, which means 'horsemen'. The Parliamentarians became known as Roundheads, because of their short hair. Both were insults given by the opponents of each side.

Early battles

The first major battle of the war took place at Edgehill in October 1642. Charles's basic aim was to reclaim London, and he marched from Shrewsbury with his newly raised army, but Parliamentarian forces marched out to meet him. They met at Edgehill, a few miles from Banbury. The Royalist cavalry, commanded by the King's nephew Prince Rupert, pushed back the wings of the Parliamentary army, but in the centre, the Royalist troops themselves took heavy casualties. After three hours of hard fighting, the battle ended in a stalemate. Charles could – perhaps should – have marched to London at this stage, but he was uncertain of how he would be received so chose to bide his time.

In 1643, there were victories for both sides but the King again failed to break through to

■ The key battles of the Civil War

London. Parliament made an alliance with the Scots, which posed a further threat to Charles.

The Battle of Marston Moor, 2 July 1644

The first really decisive battle of the war was at Marston Moor. Royalist forces in York under the command of the Marquess of Newcastle were being held under siege by three armies fighting for Parliament: an army of Scots under the Earl of Leven; local Yorkshire troops under Lord Fairfax and his son Sir Thomas Fairfax; and the Eastern Association Army under the Earl of Manchester. Manchester, as senior officer, commanded 28 000 men. Prince Rupert was sent by the King with a force of 14 000 to relieve York. By clever manoeuvring, Rupert's forces managed to enter York and break the siege. Prince Rupert believed his uncle the King wanted him to attack the Parliamentary forces in the north and so ordered his men out of the city, following the enemy out to the open plain of Marston Moor as the Parliamentary armies retreated. If all his forces had arrived at the moor in the morning Rupert would have been able to fall upon his enemy's rearguard with great effect, but Newcastle's infantry from York did not appear until the late afternoon. Many had been looting the abandoned Parliamentary armies' camps.

Because of the delay, Sir Thomas Fairfax was able to send word for the Parliamentary armies to turn around. By the time Newcastle's men had joined the Royalist ranks, the three Parliamentary armies had lined up facing them along a ridge. Rupert had his troops placed in the standard formation of the time with his cavalry on both flanks and his infantry in the centre. In front of his position ran a ditch for much of the way, in some places with a hedge. Here Rupert placed musketeers to fire upon any advancing enemy.

Upon the ridgeline opposite the Royalist army the Parliamentary forces also lined up with cavalry on the flank and infantry in the centre. Although the Royalists were outnumbered by 10 000 men, many of the Parliamentary troops were not experienced or well trained.

Civil War soldiers

The matchlock musket was the main weapon for most of the infantry on both sides. It fired a heavy lead ball loaded into the muzzle and was not very accurate, so it needed to be fired in volleys. The musket had a range of up to 91 metres, and could normally be fired once a minute. However, the black gunpowder was easily spoilt by the damp, and if the ball was not tapped firmly down the barrel it had little velocity when fired. The match, a piece of cord burning at one end, was used to ignite the powder. If the musketeer was not careful, there was a definite danger of its unintentionally setting off the powder charges he carried. When fighting hand to hand, most musketeers simply turned their matchlocks around and used them as clubs.

The other infantry weapon was the pike. The pike was a 5.5-metre pole, topped with a spear head, but was so cumbersome to carry and use that most pikemen cut down the pole by as much as a metre. The pike was used in mass formation, both against cavalry and other pikemen. When cavalry attacked, the musketeers, who usually lined up on both sides of the pike block in battle, would retreat behind the protection of the pikes and continue to fire from this position. When attacked by other infantry, the pike would be levelled as the two sides crunched together and each side tried to spear the other.

■ A matchlock musket as used by the troops during the Civil War

The cavalry provided the mobile shock troops of the Civil War battlefield. Both sides were similarly equipped, wearing heavy buff leather coats and a metal breastplate in order to deflect the enemy's swords. Most wore helmets that covered the head and neck, and had bars to protect the face. The main weapons of the cavalry were pistols and

■ Civil War pikemen, as depicted by a re-enactment group

101

swords. Cavalrymen were often trained to trot up to the enemy and fire their gun before using their sword. In spite of what most films show, the cavalry did not charge headlong into battle. Instead, the long lines of horsemen tried to stay together by first walking, and then trotting – only galloping the last few metres towards the enemy. The problem in many of the cavalry battles was that once one side broke and fled, the other side tended to chase them or go to plunder the opponents' baggage train, rather than reform and take further part in the battle. Oliver Cromwell, a Puritan Member of Parliament and farmer who had shown a natural talent for war, had trained his Parliamentary horsemen to be more disciplined in battle, earning them the name 'Ironsides'. At Marston Moor, Cromwell and his Ironsides were lined up on the left flank of the Parliamentary army, facing Prince Rupert's own horse.

The start of the battle

The two sides remained immobile, facing each other during the afternoon as rain fell off and on. In the Parliamentary ranks some began to sing Psalms. Rupert, convinced that no fighting would occur that day, had retired for supper and many of his soldiers were beginning to relax and settle for the evening.

At 7.30 p.m., just as the skies turned black and there was a loud clap of thunder, the Parliamentary line began to march down the ridge towards the Royalists. On the Parliamentary left, Cromwell led his cavalry into a charge against the Royalist cavalry, who counter-charged him. In the swirling cavalry battle the Royalists were forced to pull back, although Cromwell received a cut to his neck and had to leave the field to have it treated. Meanwhile Prince Rupert rode up and 'met his own regiment turning their backs to the enemy, which was a thing so strange and unusual he said "Swounds, do you run? Follow me!" So with them facing about, he led them to a charge ...' But Scottish reinforcements for the Parliamentarians destroyed the Prince's efforts. Rupert was unhorsed and forced to hide in a bean field for the rest of the battle. His dog, a poodle called Boy who had followed his master into many battles, was slain.

The crisis for Parliament

The battle was not going so well for Parliament on its right flank. Sir Thomas Fairfax's cavalry had found it difficult to get clear of the ditch and hedges, and the Royalist cavalry had routed it. But the Royalist commander could not keep control of his men, and many broke ranks, chasing after the enemy horses or towards the baggage train.

In the centre, even though greatly outnumbered, the Royalist foot soldiers were pushing back the Parliamentarians. As one eyewitness wrote, 'The smoke of powder was so thick that we saw no light but what proceeded from the mouth of gunnes.' Many of the Scottish and English Parliamentary soldiers feared all was lost, and fled from the battlefield.

Even some of the Parliamentary commanders believed this; Lord Fairfax apparently rode home and went to bed. Sir Thomas Fairfax, however, had not given up. He had been wounded in the face during the fighting and found himself behind the Royalist lines. As neither side at that time had a standard uniform and all spoke the same language, each side would often wear a field sign like a twig in a hat or a band of cloth to show whose side they were on. Fairfax removed the white cloth band from his hat that marked him out as a Parliamentarian, and managed to work his way around the back of the Royalist army to rejoin Cromwell's men on the left flank. Cromwell had returned to his command, which – thanks to his strict training – were still together and ready to fight. Together Cromwell and Fairfax turned the Ironsides against the Royalist infantry. As Cromwell wrote after the battle:

God made them as stubble to our swords. We charged their regiments of foot with our horse, and routed all we charged.

The stand of the Whitecoats

As the Royalist foot soldiers and cavalry ran from the battlefield, the Marquess of Newcastle's infantry regiment, known as the Whitecoats, refused to retreat and held out in a walled enclosure for an hour against the Parliamentary cavalry. Finally, as we are told by one contemporary, 'When all their ammunition was spent, having refused quarter, every man fell in the same order and rank wherein he had fought.' The sacrifice of the Whitecoats had bought time for the Royalist survivors to retreat, but around 4000 dead, wounded or captured soldiers had been left on the battlefield. Parliament losses were about 1000 men.

Results of the battle

The defeat of Prince Rupert's army dealt a tremendous blow to the Royalist cause. York fell almost immediately and there remained no large Royalist force in the north. Rupert gathered the survivors and marched west, but many of his best soldiers and officers had fallen at Marston Moor. In disgust, Newcastle went into exile in Germany. But Parliament's armies did not take full advantage of the situation. Instead, the Scots marched north, Manchester's men to East Anglia, and Fairfax to Yorkshire. Until Parliament could create a

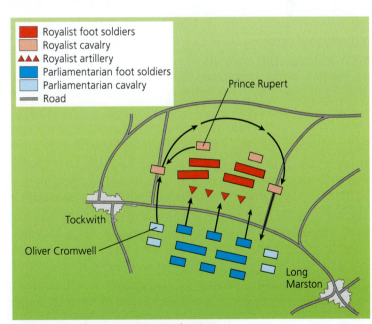

■ The Battle of Marston Moor, 2 July 1644

Royalist foot soldiers
Royalist cavalry
▲▲▲ Royalist artillery
Parliamentarian foot soldiers
Parliamentarian cavalry
Road

Prince Rupert

Tockwith

Oliver Cromwell

Long Marston

permanent force that was not divided by men from several regions, no real knockout blow could be delivered against the King.

The New Model Army

Oliver Cromwell played a major role in convincing Parliament to create a permanent, or standing, army. Between 1644 and 1645, Sir Thomas Fairfax set up the New Model Army to fight for the Parliamentarian cause, and Cromwell was chosen to command the cavalry. Fairfax and Cromwell instilled discipline into their men and told them that they were fighting to do God's will. In the words of the time:

What are the principall things required in a Souldier

1. *That he be religious and godly.*
2. *That he be courageous and valiant.*
3. *That he be skilfull in the Militarie Profession …*

■ A seventeenth-century portrait of Oliver Cromwell by Robert Walker

Anyone found guilty of indiscipline or plundering would be punished. Cromwell trained all his cavalry to advance into battle at a trot, rather than a gallop, as this allowed him to maintain control and press home his advantage, as he had done at Marston Moor. The New Model Army was also marked out by a uniform appearance. All foot soldiers were issued with red coats – this being the cheapest colour dye that could be found. However, only some of the men of the New Model Army were experienced veterans, as both sides by this stage of the war had been forced to conscript men into the ranks.

The New Model Army faced their first real test at the Battle of Naseby in June 1645. The Royalist army had captured Leicester, and when Fairfax and Cromwell advanced to meet it, the cavalry, led by Prince Rupert, attacked. Just like at Marston Moor, the Royalist cavalry charged far too quickly. The Royalist infantry, who were generally more experienced at this point, at first drove back the larger number of Parliamentary foot soldiers, again just like at Marston Moor. But the Parliamentarians then stiffened and, joined with Cromwell's cavalry from the other flank, crushed the Royalist infantry. At the last moment the King seemed ready to lead a final charge, but was persuaded not to, and fled. In the rout that followed, the King lost his private papers, which revealed that, in his desperation, he was trying to get help from France and Ireland. Probably he was willing to come to any arrangement that would bring help to his cause, but the lack of sincerity on his part is made clear in a letter which he wrote to his wife:

[I have proposed] the business of Ireland, but only in case there be no other way to save the Crown of England (for which at all times it must be sacrificed).

In 1646, Charles surrendered to the Scottish army, which sold him to the English Parliament for £400 000 the following year. The war appeared to be over. An offer was made to the King under which Parliament would continue to control the army for ten years, after which it would pass back to the Crown. Charles refused to accept the proposal, and managed to escape to the Isle of Wight – where he was promptly imprisoned in Carisbrooke Castle by the Parliamentary Governor.

While a prisoner, Charles began secret negotiations with the Scots, and agreed a treaty with the Scottish Presbyterians. Through this action Charles managed to restart the conflict, and it was this that later persuaded Cromwell that he had to be executed. In 1648, the Scots invaded England but were defeated at Preston. Parliament had finally won the Civil War.

Why did Parliament win?

There were several reasons for the Parliamentarian victory:

- The King had rich supporters but they ran out of money. Most gentlemen in areas he controlled refused to give him any money. His soldiers at the Battle of Naseby were badly equipped compared with those of Parliament. After this defeat, Charles could not afford to raise another army.
- The navy supported Parliament, which made it much more difficult for Charles to get men and supplies from abroad.
- Charles placed Prince Rupert in command of his armies. Rupert was talented and brilliant at cavalry battles, but he was inexperienced with sieges and infantry tactics.
- Parliament controlled the south-east of England, the richest part of the country. This meant it was able to finance the war. Pym had set up a well-organised system to supply Parliament's army with money.
- Parliament had a better-trained army and chose better commanders, including Oliver Cromwell and Sir Thomas Fairfax. Fairfax had been a soldier before the Civil War and commanded great respect.
- Charles left London at the very start of the Civil War, which meant that Parliament controlled the capital with all of its resources and communications, and its strategic position.
- The Royalists had a poor strategy of warfare. Charles's failure to take London after the Battle of Edgehill was a serious error.

Exercise 7.1

1 Give brief details of the following battles, saying how they were important in the Civil War:

   (a) Edgehill

   (b) Marston Moor

   (c) Naseby

2 Write a few sentences about each of the following:

   (a) Sir Thomas Fairfax

   (b) Prince Rupert

   (c) Oliver Cromwell

3 Imagine that you are a soldier fighting either on the Royalist or the Parliamentarian side at the Battle of Marston Moor. Write two letters, one on the eve of the battle and one on the day after the battle, relating your experiences.

4 Explain why the Parliamentarian army won the Battle of Marston Moor.

5 Look again at the material above on the English Civil War. Explain why the Parliamentarian side won.

The trial of Charles I

Once the Parliamentarian forces had won the Civil War, the difficult question arose of what to do with the King. Most MPs believed that they should negotiate with him, even if they were forced to concede to him on some of his demands. But others, led by Oliver Cromwell, believed that Charles could not be trusted. They had offered him terms before, and he had refused them. Now was not the time to be generous.

In what became known as 'Pride's Purge', the Parliamentarian army surrounded the House of Commons on 6 December 1648. Only MPs who supported putting Charles on trial were allowed in; the rest were barred from entering. In this way, 231 MPs were excluded, and the remaining 240 took up their places in what came to be known as the Rump Parliament. On 1 January 1649, they voted to put the King on trial.

There were several charges against Charles:

● As king, he had been trusted to govern England according to the law, but instead had made himself a tyrant, ruling according to his own will rather than according to the law.

- He had made war on his own subjects, and was therefore responsible for all the crimes committed in his name.
- He had asked for help against his own subjects from the French and the Dutch.
- He had restarted the war against Parliament and the people after surrendering.

Charles refused to answer the charges, arguing that the court had no right to try him. He said he was the lawful king, responsible to God, and could not be brought to trial by his subjects. Neither he nor the House of Lords had agreed to the setting up of the court. He also said that the real power behind the court was the army, not the law or the rights of the people.

A panel of 135 special judges, called commissioners, was appointed to try the King, but of these, only 80 took part in the trial. They were led by John Bradshaw – who wore a bulletproof hat throughout. Charles was found guilty of treason by 68 of the judges, 59 of whom signed the death warrant. This was an astounding move. Kings had been killed in battle or murdered before, but no king had ever been put on trial and then executed. All of Europe was amazed at the event.

The execution of Charles I

Charles said, just before his execution, 'I want the people's freedom as much as anyone, but I must tell you that freedom means having a government and laws. It does not mean the people having a share in government.'

It was very cold on the morning of 30 January 1649. Charles asked his servant for a second shirt in case people saw him shivering and thought he was afraid. 'I fear not death,' he said. He walked calmly to the Banqueting House at the Palace of Whitehall. At one o'clock, he stepped through the open window and on to the scaffold. 'I am a martyr to the people,' he shouted. Then he knelt at the block and, with one blow of the axe, his head was cut off.

An eyewitness wrote this account of the execution:

I was in the crowd in the street before Whitehall gate where the scaffold was, and saw what was done, but was not so near as to hear anything. I saw the blow given. At that moment, I remember, there was such a groan from the crowd as I never heard before and I hope I never hear again. There was, as ordered, one troop of soldiers immediately marching to scatter the people, so I had to move quickly to get home without hurt.

■ The execution of Charles I; from a painting produced around 1649 by an unknown artist. The painting includes four small pictures as follows: Charles (top left); Charles walking to the execution (bottom left); the executioner holding up Charles's head (top right); and people dipping their handkerchiefs in his blood (bottom right). These bloody handkerchiefs were later said by Charles's supporters to have caused miraculous cures from illnesses.

Charles's head was later sewn back on to his body, and he was buried in St George's Chapel, Windsor.

Exercise 7.2

1 Copy and complete the following table, perhaps as part of a class discussion. Then answer the question below the table.

Charges against Charles I	Evidence for guilt	Evidence for innocence
Ruled as a tyrant.		
Made war on his own subjects.		
Asked for help from the French and the Dutch.		
Restarted the war after surrendering.		

Was Charles I guilty of the crimes he was charged with at his trial? Explain your answer.

2 Read the eyewitness account of the execution (page 107). How does the author describe the crowd's reaction, and what is his attitude to the events he describes? Write a few sentences to explain.

In some branches of the Church of England, 30 January is celebrated as the feast day of 'Charles I, King and martyr'. In this way he is commemorated in the same way as a saint. Why do you think this is?

3 Imagine you were an eyewitness at the execution of Charles I. Write an account of what you heard, saw and smelt that day.

The Rump Parliament

After the execution of King Charles I, the Rump Parliament (see page 106) declared England to be a commonwealth, meaning that the wealth of the country would be used for the common good. The monarchy and House of Lords were abolished and, to help in the running of the country, a Council of State was set up. The members of the council were chosen from the 70 or so MPs in the Rump. Meanwhile, the real power in the land lay with the army and Oliver Cromwell.

The Rump Parliament set out to address some of the problems that had existed under Charles, but it turned out to be remarkably ineffective. It introduced some degree of religious toleration, allowing independent churches to exist alongside those of the established Church, although all still had to pay their **tithes** to the Church of England. There were some minor changes to the legal system, such as requiring all proceedings to be conducted in English rather than Welsh or Cornish. However, Cromwell soon grew tired of Parliament's inability to carry through the radical reforms he was pressing for, and on 20 April 1653 he dissolved the Rump, saying:

You have sat here too long for any good you have been doing. Depart I say, and let us have done with you. In the name of God, go!

Later that year when justifying his actions, Cromwell said that he had been carrying out God's will:

When I went there [to Parliament], I did not think to have done this. But perceiving the spirit of God so strong upon me, I would not consult flesh and blood.

Barebone's Parliament

Cromwell claimed that he did not want a military dictatorship in England and he sought to set up a 'Parliament of the Saints', a body based on the values of the Bible that would introduce reforms to address the issues facing England after the Civil War. The new assembly was nicknamed Barebone's Parliament after one of its members, who had the unlikely name of Praise-God Barebone.

Cromwell tried to work with religious leaders to work out a plan for 'a godly commonwealth', but the various groups found it impossible to work together. In December 1653, Parliament decided to surrender its responsibilities to Cromwell. The Speaker and some 40 MPs walked to Cromwell's residence at Whitehall where they formally handed their authority to him. Having spent so many years resisting the efforts of one man, the king, from imposing his will on their house, MPs seem to have decided that the concept of a sole ruler was one they liked, or at least understood. Not all the MPs went along with this, but Cromwell sent his soldiers in to clear out any who resisted him.

Exercise 7.3

1 Why did Cromwell dissolve the Rump Parliament? Write a few sentences to explain.

2 Why do you think the members of Barebone's Parliament handed their authority over to Cromwell? Write a few sentences to explain.

Oliver Cromwell, Lord Protector, 1653–58

Cromwell believed that the victory of the New Model Army in the Civil War had been God's will, and therefore that it was God's will that he should be Lord Protector, or ruler. He was appointed to this position on 16 December 1653, after the dissolution of Barebone's Parliament.

Cromwell set out to rule with a Council of State and Parliament. He accepted the existence of an established Church, but no one was compelled to attend it. Under Cromwell, Catholics and Jews were able to worship freely in private, without fear of arrest. However, his plans for the new Parliament failed and when tensions grew, with threats of Royalist uprisings, he resorted to rule by the army.

In 1655, he divided England into eleven districts and appointed a Major-General to administer each one and to impose law and order. Unlawful assemblies were banned, robbers and vagrants were arrested and former Royalist sympathisers were disarmed. A new ten per cent tax called the **decimation tax** was imposed to finance the raising of local armies in each of the districts.

In 1657, Cromwell called a meeting of army officers to discuss a new constitution for England. Thomas Burton was at the meeting, and reported:

One hundred officers said to His Highness [Cromwell] that he should not take the title of King because it was not pleasing to his army, it was a matter of scandal to the people of God, it was dangerous to his own person, and it would make way for Charles Stuart to come in again.

But while there was a feeling that Cromwell should not be seen as a replacement for the monarch they had removed, the new constitution of 1657 put in place arrangements for a magnificent ceremony to acknowledge Cromwell's position as Lord Protector; and decreed that Cromwell's son, Richard, would succeed him in the role. It must have seemed to some that one type of hereditary ruler had been replaced by another. After a final attempt to use Parliament, Cromwell ruled with the aid of the army for the last month of his life.

Exercise 7.4

SOURCE A: An extract from a letter by Lorenzo Paulucci, the Venetian ambassador to London, in 1653.

Such are the principal contents of the Instrument of Government that for all practical purposes it makes him [Cromwell] king; indeed giving him more than sovereign authority... Although England has had Protectors before, she never made them as absolute as this.

SOURCE B: A description of Cromwell's investiture as Lord Protector in June 1657. The origin of the source is unknown.

As he entered Westminster Hall, His Highness was dressed in a robe of purple velvet lined with ermine, being the dress used at the investiture of princes.

SOURCE C: A Dutch cartoon of Cromwell as king (below right); produced in 1658.

1 In Source A, what is Paulucci suggesting about Cromwell's rule?

2 Cromwell refused the throne in 1653. What does Source B show about his attitude to ruling England four years later?

3 Source C is a cartoon poking fun at Cromwell. How does this source help us to understand the changing role of Cromwell?

4 Using all the sources and your own knowledge, how far do you agree that Oliver Cromwell did not want to be a king?

◯ The conquest of Ireland

To ensure the security of the new regime, the English Parliament had to deal with any possible threats from Ireland and Scotland. These were separate countries from England, but had all been ruled by Charles I. Now that Parliament had abolished the monarchy, Ireland and Scotland were entirely independent of England.

The Irish had rebelled after the execution of Charles in 1649. Parliament thought the Irish rebels might join Charles's son and attempt to restore the monarchy. Cromwell took a force of soldiers to Ireland in the summer of 1649 and, having occupied Dublin, he moved on to the town of Drogheda, a Catholic stronghold on the road to Ulster. In September, Cromwell assaulted the town, and about 3500 civilians and soldiers were killed. Parliamentarian losses totalled about 150 men. Cromwell

■ Dutch cartoon of Cromwell as king, 1658

saw the victory as God's punishment of the Catholics for having rebelled. After the capture of Drogheda, he said:

This is a righteous judgement of God upon these barbarous wretches, who have imbued their hands in so much innocent blood ...

The following month, the port of Wexford was captured, and about 1500 civilians were killed. Once again, Cromwell felt that God was punishing the Catholics. The rebellion was crushed and Cromwell returned to England in early 1650. The rebels' land was divided among Cromwell's followers, stirring up many problems for Ireland in the years ahead.

The conquest of Scotland

On his return from Ireland, Cromwell was faced with problems in Scotland. The Scots accepted Charles I's son as their rightful king, and crowned him as Charles II. Cromwell's dilemma was that he had to face not Catholics this time, but Scottish Presbyterians, radical Protestants similar to the Puritans. He wrote a letter to the General Assembly of Scotland about the alliance with Charles, saying:

I beseech you, in the bowels of Christ, think it possible you may be mistaken.

The Scots were unmoved and Cromwell marched north. The two armies met at Dunbar on 3 September 1650, and Cromwell was victorious. In December he captured Edinburgh. Cromwell called the victory 'a high act of the Lord's Providence to us, and one of the most signal mercies God hath done for England and His people'. Nevertheless, Charles and the Scots fought on and in 1651, their forces moved south into England with Cromwell in pursuit. The final confrontation came on 3 September at the Battle of Worcester, which was fought through the streets of the town, and the Royalists were defeated once again. Charles escaped from the battlefield and, it is said, hid in an oak tree to escape Cromwell's soldiers as they searched for survivors. He then fled to France.

- The conquest of Ireland

Find out how Oliver Cromwell is regarded in Ireland today. Are your findings what you would expect?

- The conquest of Scotland

For the rest of the Commonwealth and Protectorate, Scotland was ruled from London and was occupied by Cromwell's army.

◯ Puritan England

Cromwell was an extremely religious man, and believed that it was God's will that Puritan values be introduced throughout the land. However, for the people to accept the Puritan way of life favoured by Cromwell and others, the entire moral framework of the country would have to be changed. Many of the laws that were introduced affected the daily lives of the ordinary people and were not popular with everyone. This is shown in a report of 1647 that was sent to the Speaker of the House of Commons. It refers to people playing football in towns in England:

Under the pretence of playing football and cudgel playing and the like, there have lately been suspicious meetings and assemblies at several places, made up of disaffected persons, and more such are planned.

Cromwell's men made sure that these 'disaffected people' were unable to cause any trouble, and a climate of fear gripped the country. Gradually, stricter codes of behaviour came to be expected, and the 'merrie England' that had existed for so long became a thing of the past. Dancing, singing, drinking, indeed nearly all forms of entertainment were banned. Clothing changed from being bright and colourful to being dark and drab. On Sundays people were allowed to do little else other than go to church and study the Bible.

Puritans even argued that Christmas was a Catholic celebration that was simply an excuse for drunkenness and gluttony. In 1652, the celebration of Christmas Day was banned:

Friday the four and 20th day of December, 1652

Resolved by the Parliament,

That the Markets be kept to Morrow, being the five and 20th day of December; and that the Lord Mayor, and Sheriffs of London and Middlesex, and the Justices of the Peace for the City of London and Westminster and Liberties thereof, do take care, that all such persons as shall open their shops on that day, be protected from wrong or violence, and the offenders be punished.

Resolved by the Parliament,

That no observations shall be had of the five and 20th day of December, commonly called Christmas-Day; nor any solemnity used or exercised in churches upon that day in respect thereof.

Ordered by Parliament,

That the Lord Mayor of the City of London and Sheriffs of London and Middlesex, and the Justices of the Peace of Middlesex respectively be Authorised and required to see this order duly observed.

The Puritans also banned maypole dancing and public recreations, such as cockfighting, bear-baiting and horse racing. Gambling dens, theatres and inns were closed down.

Of course, the extent to which these changes affected people was different from region to region. But certainly the England of the 1650s was a very different place, in so many ways, from that of the 1600s.

■ A seventeenth-century portrait of a Puritan family

Exercise 7.5

Explain how the Puritans changed English life at this time.

Tumble-down Dick

When Oliver Cromwell died on 3 September 1658, his son Richard became Lord Protector of England. Richard was not suited to the task – not being a military commander, he had no support from the army. Furthermore, he immediately faced a serious financial problem: a national debt of about £2 million inherited from his father. It was like the bad old days of the monarchy again. Cromwell needed money and the only solution was to call Parliament. He demanded higher taxes to fund the army, but Parliament was reluctant to agree, being more keen on restricting the army's power. Parliament and the army could not agree and, in May 1659, Richard resigned as Lord Protector.

After his resignation, Royalists nicknamed Richard Cromwell 'Tumble-down Dick'. He went into exile the following year and did not return to England for twenty years. He died in 1712.

Exercise 7.6

SOURCE A: From the obituary of Oliver Cromwell, published in the *Commonwealth Mercury*, 3 September 1658.

His most Serene and Renowned Highness OLIVER Lord Protector, being after a sickness of about fourteen days (which appeared an ague in the beginning) reduced to a very low condition of Body, began early this morning to draw near the gate of death; and it pleased God about three o'clock … to put a period to his life. I would express upon this sad occasion, the deep sorrow which hath possessed the minds of his most Noble Son and Successor, and other dearest relations, had I language sufficient: but all that I can use will fall short of the merits of that most excellent Prince.

SOURCE B: From the writings of John Milton, who served in Cromwell's government.

Our country owes its liberties to you … you are the author, the guardian, and the preserver of our liberties; and you have eclipsed not only the achievements of all our kings, but also even our legendary heroes … You hold the sceptre over three powerful nations, to persuade people to give up indecent and corrupt morals for more noble behaviour …

SOURCE C: The statue of Oliver Cromwell at Westminster, London. It was erected in 1899.

■ Statue of Oliver Cromwell, Westminster

1 Read Source A. What is the writer's opinion of Oliver Cromwell?

2 How useful are Sources A and B as evidence of the work of Cromwell?

3 Look at Source C. Why do you think Cromwell's statue was placed next to the Houses of Parliament at Westminster?

4 Using all the sources and your own knowledge, how far do you agree that Cromwell deserved the praise he received after his death?

The Restoration

After Richard Cromwell's resignation as Lord Protector, Parliament and the army tried to run the country but fell into constant squabbles. In the autumn of 1659, General George Monck, who commanded the large army in Scotland, led his men south. As Monck's forces moved towards London, his opponents melted away. In December 1659, the Long Parliament was recalled, some of whose members were in favour of restoring the monarchy. This Parliament had never been dissolved since it was first assembled in 1640, which is why it earned its name. The general feeling was that in order to preserve stability and ensure that there was not another civil war, there had to be unity around one figure. Restoring the monarchy under Charles Stuart, the son of Charles I, was considered the best option.

Monck began negotiations with Charles's advisors in March 1660, and the following month, Charles issued the Declaration of Breda. This guaranteed:

- a free Parliament
- fair pay for soldiers
- land rights and pardons for those who had fought against the Crown in the Civil War.

This pardon was to be extended to all apart from those involved in the **regicide** itself (the killing of the king).

For his part, Charles agreed to accept the limits placed on the Crown in 1641.

Here is an extract from the text of the Declaration of Breda:

Charles, by the Grace of God, King of England, Scotland, France and Ireland, Defender of the Faith, to all our loving subjects ... If the general distraction and confusion which is spread over the whole kingdom doth not awaken all men to a desire and longing that those wounds which have so many years together been kept bleeding, may be bound up, all we can say will be to no purpose; however, after this long silence, we have thought it our duty to declare how much we desire to contribute thereunto; and to the end that the fear of punishment may not engage any ... we do grant a free and general pardon ... excepting only such persons as shall hereby be excepted by Parliament ... we are desiring and ordaining that henceforth all notes of discord, separation and difference of parties be utterly abolished among all our subjects, whom we invite and conjure to a perfect union among themselves, under our protection, for the resettlement of our just rights and theirs in a free Parliament, by which upon the word of a king, we will be advised.

Parliament declared Charles II to be king on 8 May 1660. The new king entered London on 29 May, his 30th birthday, and was crowned the following year.

■ Charles Stuart in Whitehall, London, 29 May 1660; a painting by Isaac Fuller, c.1660

The period 1649–60 is referred to in three ways. First there was the period of commonwealth, when government was for the common good of the people; then there was the protectorate, when England was governed by a Lord Protector. The whole period was an **interregnum**. This is a Latin word meaning 'between reigns'. But by 1660, all that was a thing of the past: the body of Oliver Cromwell, once seen as the saviour of England's liberties, was exhumed and hanged at Tyburn on 30 January 1661, the anniversary of Charles I's execution. The corpse was then decapitated and the skull displayed on a pole outside Westminster Abbey. The republican experiment was at an end.

Exercise 7.7

1   How successful was Oliver Cromwell as Lord Protector from 1653 to 1658?

2   Explain why England restored the monarchy in 1660.

3   Write a speech for Charles II to give to the people on his way to London in May 1660.

8 Charles II and James II

Charles II, 1660–85

Charles II sailed home to England in May 1660 and was met by crowds of happy, cheering people. Samuel Pepys, the famous diarist, was in the fleet of ships that accompanied Charles and he recorded the event in his diary for 25 May:

I went [to accompany the King to the shore] with a dog that the King loved ... and so got on shore when the King did, who was received by General Monck with all imaginable love and respect at his entrance upon the land at Dover. Infinite the crowd of people and the gallantry of the horsemen, citizens, and noblemen of all sorts.

To many, the restoration of the monarchy marked a return to the joyous times before the Puritans seized power, with dancing and music, theatres and feast days all becoming a part of English life once more.

Charles himself set the tone, living an extravagant life at court. He married Catherine of Braganza in 1662 but kept a string of mistresses, most famously the actress Nell Gwynn, and fathered at least fourteen illegitimate children. The Puritans (from this time generally referred to as 'non-conformists' or 'dissenters') attacked the so-called 'Merrie Monarch' for his lack of morals, calling him 'that great enemy of chastity and marriage'. Life under Charles II appeared carefree and fun. The Earl of Rochester, who knew Charles well, is said to have made the following rhyme about him:

We have a pretty witty king,

Whose word no man relies on;

He never said a foolish thing,

Nor ever did a wise one.

■ Charles II at his coronation; a painting from the studio of Michael Wright, c.1660

And speaking about Charles II around 1713, the Bishop of Salisbury said:

He had a softness of temper that charmed all who came near him, till they found out how little they could depend on good looks, kind words and fair promises. He was friendly and easy-going. He was an everlasting talker. He seemed to have no sense of religion.

The regicides

Although Charles was prepared to pardon those who had fought against his father during the Civil War, he was determined to punish those responsible for his death – not only the 59 commissioners who had condemned Charles I, but also the officials who had participated in the events leading to the execution. By the time of the Restoration, twenty of the commissioners had died, but the remainder were tried and found guilty of regicide, and were either executed or imprisoned. The bodies of three of the commissioners who had already died were exhumed and their bodies hanged.

> **Find out as much as you can about how the regicides were regarded after the Restoration. Why were the bodies of Cromwell, and the other regicides who had since died, treated in such a manner?**

Exercise 8.1

1 Write a few sentences to explain the meaning of the following:

   (a) The Restoration

   (b) Dissenters

   (c) Regicides

2 Write a newspaper headline and leading article about the Restoration. Ensure the headline is striking, and then highlight issues of the past, present and future.

3 Why do you think Charles II was hated by Puritans? Consider his behaviour, and the regime he replaced. Write a paragraph to explain.

The Convention and Cavalier Parliaments

The elections of 1660 had produced a Royalist Parliament, full of men who had wanted Charles to become king. The **Convention Parliament**, as it was called, sat until the end of 1660 and its work of dismantling all the Acts of Parliament and institutions set up during the Commonwealth and Protectorate was continued by the **Cavalier Parliament**, elected in May 1661. The Cavalier Parliament sat until 1679. It was overwhelmingly Royalist and very supportive of Charles.

With Parliament on his side, Charles II set about restoring the power of the monarchy, which had been so violently challenged in the reign of his father.

119

- Control of the army was handed back to the King.
- An annual grant of money was established to pay for the army's upkeep.
- The House of Lords was restored and bishops were allowed once more to take up their seats.
- The Triennial Act, which had required Parliament to meet for at least one fifty-day session every three years, was repealed.

In these ways, Charles oversaw a restoration of the power of the monarchy, but this was not universally popular. The Bishop of Salisbury noted:

He thought a king who might be checked or have his ministers called to account by a Parliament was but a king in name.

The Cavalier Parliament later started to split into two camps. One camp, which included royal courtiers such as Lord Clifford, Lord Arlington, the Earl of Buckingham and Lord Lauderdale, supported Charles, and became known as Tories. The other camp, mainly country gentlemen and self-made men, were more concerned about restricting the King's power, and became known as Whigs. These factions would later develop into political parties as we know them today.

Charles and religion

Although Charles II converted to Roman Catholicism on his deathbed, and was himself tolerant of other religions, his reign is notable for the extent to which religious toleration was ended. Most significantly, by a series of four Acts of Parliament, known as the **Clarendon Code**, the supremacy of the Anglican Church was upheld.

The Clarendon Code

The Clarendon Code was named after the Lord Chancellor, the Earl of Clarendon, even though he actually disapproved of some of its content.
- Corporation Act (1661)
  This required all municipal officials to take Anglican communion, and excluded non-conformists from public office.
- Act of Uniformity (1662)
  This made the use of the *Book of Common Prayer* compulsory in religious services. It has been estimated that about 2000 clergy refused to comply with this Act, and were forced to resign their livings.
- Conventicle Act (1664)
  This forbade **conventicles** (meetings for unauthorised worship) of more than five people who were not members of the same household.

- Five-Mile Act (1665)
  This was aimed at non-conformist ministers, who were forbidden from coming within five miles of incorporated towns or the place of their former livings. They were also forbidden to teach in schools. This Act was not repealed until 1812.

Charles and Catholicism

As his reign went on, Charles's wish to allow Roman Catholics to worship freely became stronger. In 1672, he issued a Declaration of Indulgence which, it was hoped, would give greater religious freedom not only to Catholics but also to Protestant dissenters. However, the vast majority of MPs remained strict Protestants and their reaction to the Declaration of Indulgence was to pass the Test Act of 1673. This Act required all government officials to swear an oath that they were Protestants. Several of the King's senior ministers were forced to resign and religious tension continued to grow.

■ The plague spread rapidly through the city

○ The Great Plague, 1665

England, then, had turned its back on the austere years of Puritan rule, and people were once more able to enjoy themselves in public without running the risk of being arrested. However, this sense of joy was abruptly ended in London with a serious outbreak of plague. A plague which had spread across western Europe in 1663, came to London in 1664 and in 1665 took hold of the city. The official death toll in the city was 68 576, but the true figure was probably nearer 100 000. The plague was spread by rat fleas, and the rats were attracted by the domestic waste and human sewage that were to be found throughout the city. The summer of 1665 was one of the hottest for years, and this was another factor behind the rapid spread of the plague.

The King and the royal court moved to Hampton Court Palace, and later to Oxford, while the nobility fled the city to live on their estates in the country. Suffering was on a huge scale and ordinary life came to a halt.

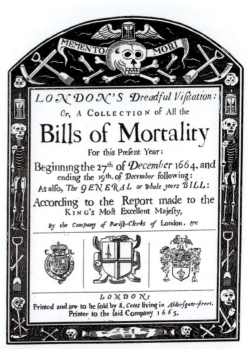

LONDON'S Dreadful Visitation:
Or, A Collection of All the
Bills of Mortality
For this Present Year:
Beginning the 27th of December 1664. and ending the 19th. of December following:
As also, The GENERAL or whole years BILL:
According to the Report made to the King's Most Excellent Majesty,
By the Company of Parish-Clerks of London, &c

LONDON:
Printed and are to be fold by E. Cotes living in Aldersgate-street. Printer to the faid Company 1665.

■ The Bills of Mortality for London during 1665. Each parish produced its own Bill of Mortality, which showed the manner in which people had died.

Samuel Pepys, who was working at the Navy Board in London during these years, kept a diary for the period 1660–69, and his record of the plague makes for grim reading:

7th June This day I did in Drury Lane see two or three houses marked with a red cross upon their doors and 'Lord have mercy upon us' writ there, which was a sad sight to me.

21st June I found all the town almost going out of town, the coaches and wagons being all full of people going into the country.

31st August Up, and after putting several things in order to my removal to Woolwich, the plague having a great increase this week beyond all expectation, of almost 2,000 – making the general Bill 7,000 and the plague above 6,000 ... Thus this month ends, with great sadness upon the public through the greatness of the plague, everywhere through the Kingdom almost. Every day sadder and sadder news of its increase. In the City died this week 7,496; and of them, 6,102 of the plague. But it is feared that the true number of the dead this week is near 10,000 – partly from the poor that cannot be taken notice of through the greatness of the number, and partly from the Quakers and others that will not have any bell ring for them.

20th September But, Lord! What a sad time it is to see no boats on the river, and the grass grows all up and down Whitehall court and nobody but poor wretches on the streets.

31st December It is true we have gone through great melancholy because of the great plague, and I put to great charges by it, by keeping my family long at Woolwich, and myself and another part of my family, my clerks at my charge at Greenwich, and a maid at London. But now the plague is abated almost to nothing.

The Lord Mayor issued specific instructions to all Londoners to prevent the spread of the plague:

- Infected houses had to be marked with a red cross on which the words 'Lord have mercy upon us' had to be inscribed.
- No person could leave an infected house for at least a month after it was found to be infected. Watchmen were appointed to guard infected houses – one for the day and one for the night.
- Women searchers were appointed to patrol the streets, monitor the deaths and report the causes of death. These searchers were not allowed to keep a shop or work as a laundress.

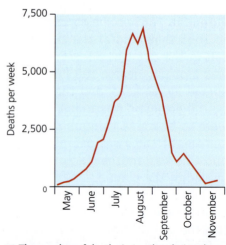
■ The number of deaths in London during the plague in 1665

- The dead were to be buried after sunset and before sunrise.
- No pigs, dogs, cats or rabbits were to be kept in the city.

Daniel Defoe, in his *Journal of the Plague Year* (written in 1722), estimated that about 40 000 dogs and 200 000 cats were killed. However, killing cats and dogs proved to be a mistake as they were the animals that killed the rats.

The plague ravaged the city until October, when at last it began to pass, as the cold weather helped to kill it off. However, it was not until February 1666 that King Charles considered it safe to return to the city.

Exercise 8.2

1 Explain the effect the 1665 plague had on life in London.

2 Write an account of the plague as if you were living and working in London.

Exercise 8.3

SOURCE A: From J.P. Kenyon's *Stuart England*, published in 1978.

The Plague and the Fire had a disastrous effect on public morale. The epidemic of bubonic plague in the summer of 1665 was the worst in the century: it killed about 70,000 Londoners and paralysed the port for six months. The Great Fire of September 1666 was probably less damaging, but it was more spectacular, and it left its mark on the City for at least another twenty years.

SOURCE B: A modern account of the plague, from the Harvard University Library Open Collections Program.

First suspected in late 1664, London's plague began to spread in earnest eastwards in April 1665 from the destitute suburb of St Giles through rat-infested alleys to the crowded and squalid parishes of Whitechapel and Stepney on its way to the walled City of London.

By September 1665, the death rate had reached 8,000 per week. Helpless municipal authorities threw their earlier caution to the wind and abandoned quarantine measures. Houses containing the dead and dying were no longer locked. London's mournful silence was broken by the noise of carts carrying the dead for burial in parish churches or communal plague pits such as Finsbury Field in Cripplegate and the open fields in Southwark.

SOURCE C: From the *Journal of the Plague Year* by Daniel Defoe, published in 1722.

This [a report of the plague] turned the people's eyes pretty much towards that end of the town, and the weekly bills showing an increase of burials in St Giles's parish more than usual, it began to be suspected that the plague was among the people at that end of the town, and that many had died of it, though they had taken care to keep it as much from the knowledge of the public as possible. People were very worried, and few cared to go through Drury Lane, or the other streets suspected, unless they had extraordinary business that obliged them to go there.

This increase of the bills stood thus: the usual number of burials in a week, in the parishes of St Giles-in-the-Fields and St Andrew's, Holborn, were from twelve to seventeen or nineteen each, few more or less; but from the time that the plague first began in St Giles's parish, it was observed that the ordinary burials increased in number considerably.

1　What can you learn from Source A about the plague of 1665?

2　What does Source B tell you about how the people of London tried to control the plague?

3　How far does Source C agree with the information given in Sources A and B?

4　Using all the sources and your own knowledge, how far do you agree that the plague of 1665 was the greatest disaster for London in the seventeenth century?

The Great Fire of London, 1666

■ The Great Fire of London; from a painting completed in 1666 by Lieve Verschuier; the Tower of London is on the right and St Paul's is in the distance surrounded by the tallest flames.

The next disaster to hit London was the Great Fire of 1666. Fires in England's towns and cities were quite common in the seventeenth century. Buildings were largely made of wood and packed closely together, which made them very vulnerable. However, the Great Fire of London was different because of its scale, duration and intensity. It began early on Sunday morning, 2 September 1666, and lasted for four days and nights. It began in Pudding Lane at the bakery of Thomas Farynor, baker to the King, whose ovens had not been sufficiently checked before bed.

After the long, hot summer of 1666, the wooden buildings of London were tinder dry. The fire spread quickly through the wooden houses of Pudding Lane and soon reached the riverside wharves, which were full of such items as timber, hay, oil, tallow and coal, all piled up ready for export. From here the fire exploded into the city, as sparks were carried long distances to set whole streets ablaze. There was no fire brigade in those days, and the citizen firefighters only had access to buckets and hooks on long poles to fight the blaze. Thanks to this, and the refusal of many house owners to have their homes pulled down, there was no containing the fire and it continued to spread. What was needed to contain the blaze was a prompt decision to set up firebreaks; but the Lord Mayor failed to give this. By the time the decision was taken to pull houses down (thereby creating firebreaks) it was too late for much of the city. Finally the King and his brother, the Duke of York, stepped in and used gunpowder to create firebreaks around the Tower of London. The fire blazed for five days before it died as the strong easterly winds eased.

As with the plague in the previous year, the diary of Samuel Pepys is a vivid source of information about the Great Fire:

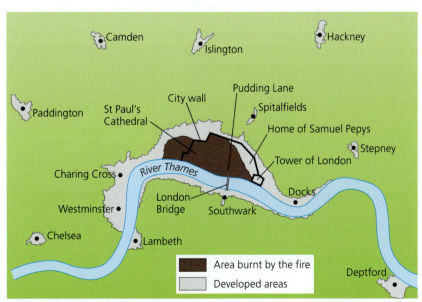

■ The area of London affected by the Great Fire in 1666

2nd September *Jane called us up about three in the morning, to tell us of a great fire they saw in the City. So I rose and slipped on my nightgown, and went to her window, and thought it to be on the backside of Marke-lane at the farthest; but, being unused to such fires as followed, I thought it far enough off; and so went to bed again and to sleep. About seven, rose again to dress myself, and there looked out at the window, and saw the fire not so much as it was and further off. So to my closet to set things to rights after yesterday's cleansing. By and by Jane comes and tells me that she hears that above 300 houses have been burned down tonight by the fire we saw, and that it is now burning down all Fish-street, by London Bridge.*

3rd September *About four o'clock in the morning, my Lady Batten sent me a cart to carry away all my money, and plate, and best things, to Sir W. Rider's at Bednall-green. Which I did riding myself in my night-gown in the cart; and, Lord! to see how the streets and the highways are crowded with people running and riding, and getting of carts at any rate to fetch away things. I am eased at my heart to have my treasure so well secured. Then home, with much ado to find a way, nor any sleep all this night to me nor my poor wife.*

4th September *Only now and then walking into the garden, and saw how horridly the sky looks, all on a fire in the night, was enough to put us out of our wits; and, indeed, it was extremely dreadful, for it looks just as if it was at us; and the whole heaven on fire. I after supper walked in the dark down to Tower Street, and there saw it all on fire.*

5th September *Walked into Moorefields (my feet ready to burn, walking through the town among the hot coals), and find that full of people, and poor wretches carrying their goods there, and everybody keeping his goods together by themselves (and a great blessing it is to them that it is fair weather for them to keep abroad night and day). Drank there, and paid two-pence for a plain penny loaf.*

6th September *A sad sight to see how the River looks: no houses nor church near it, to the Temple, where it stopped ... But strange it was to see Clothworkers' Hall on fire these three days and nights in one body of flame, it being the cellar full of oil.*

7th September *Up by five o'clock and, blessed be God! I find all well, and by water to Paul's Wharf. Walked thence, and saw, all the town burned, and a miserable sight of Paul's church; with all the roofs fallen, and the body of the quire fallen into St Faith's. To Sir W. Coventry, at St James's ... He hopes we shall have no public distractions upon this fire, which is what everybody fears, because of the talk of the French having a hand in it. And it is a proper time for discontents; but all men's minds are full of care to protect themselves, and save their goods: the militia is in arms everywhere.*

Although few people died in the fire, more than three-quarters of the City were destroyed. About 13 000 houses and 90 churches were destroyed together with 52 guildhalls (the centres from which the rich merchants ran their businesses). Thousands of citizens were made homeless and large numbers were ruined financially.

Rebuilding began immediately, and new regulations were brought in to make future fires less likely. Some streets were widened and timber was banned for building, with red brick and white stone being used instead. More than 50 new churches were built and the famous architect Sir Christopher Wren designed a new St Paul's Cathedral.

A monument, designed by Sir Christopher Wren, was erected in London to commemorate the Great Fire of London. It was built close to the site of the bakery where the fire began, and can still be seen today.

> Several different designs were submitted by architects who wished to rebuild London. Some wanted to change the street layout radically. Find out what you can about these alternative designs.

Exercise 8.4

1 Explain why London was unable to deal effectively with the Great Fire of 1666.

2 Imagine you were living in London in 1666. Write a series of diary entries to record the events of the period 2–7 September.

The Popish Plot, 1678

Charles's brother James, who was heir to the throne, was known to be a Roman Catholic and – after the death of his first wife Anne Hyde – had married the Catholic Mary of Modena in 1673.

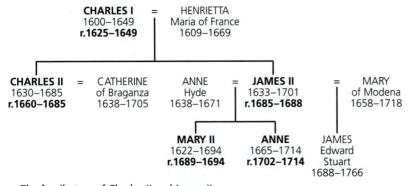

■ The family tree of Charles II and James II

In 1678, a malicious and deceitful Anglican priest named Titus Oates claimed that a plot was being hatched to murder Charles and put his Catholic brother on the throne. He said the plot involved Charles's wife and several leading Catholics.

127

Parliament was horrified and a bill was proposed by the Whigs, the Exclusion Bill, which would have excluded James from the throne, in favour of Charles's illegitimate son James, Duke of Monmouth, who was a Protestant (see family tree, page 163). The discussions over the Exclusion Bill went on for weeks, but in the end it was rejected by the House of Lords. During this time, there were anti-Catholic riots, many Catholic office-holders lost their jobs and a series of treason trials was held. Between twenty and thirty Catholics were executed and many more died in prison.

It turned out that Oates had made the story up, and in 1685 he was convicted of perjury (telling lies in court when under oath to tell the truth). Below is an extract from the court's sentence on Titus Oates:

First, the Court does order for a fine, that you pay 1,000 marks upon each Indictment. Secondly, that you be stripped of all your Canonical Habits. Thirdly, the Court does award, that you do stand upon the Pillory, and in the Pillory, here before Westminster-hall gate, upon Monday next, for an hour's time, between the hours of 10 and 12; with a paper over your head (which you must first walk with round about to all the Courts in Westminister Hall) declaring your crime. Fourthly, upon Tuesday, you shall stand upon, and in the Pillory, at the Royal Exchange in London, for the space of an hour, between the hours of twelve and two, with the same inscription. You shall upon the next Wednesday be whipped from Aldgate to Newgate. Upon Friday, you shall be whipped from Newgate to Tyburn, by the hands of the common hangman.

The unrest soon died out but anti-Catholic feelings remained and even after the crisis was over, Catholics remained excluded from Parliament.

◯ The Rye House Plot, 1683

In 1683, some Whig leaders were implicated in a plot to assassinate Charles II and his brother, James. The plot was discovered in June and some of the leaders were arrested. Whig leaders Lord William Russell and Algernon Sidney were convicted and executed, and the Earl of Essex committed suicide in the Tower of London. The plot had the effect of creating a wave of sympathy not only for Charles but also for James, who was allowed to be an advisor to his brother once more.

After the plot, Charles ruled without Parliament until the end of his reign. He died in 1685 and his brother, James II, succeeded to the throne.

Exercise 8.5

1 Write a few sentences to explain the following:

(a) The Clarendon Code

(b) The Declaration of Indulgence

(c) The Test Act

2 Explain why the Popish Plot and the Rye House Plot were important for King Charles II.

Exercise 8.6

Read the following extract, from Samuel Pepys writing about Charles II. Then look back to the statements made by the Bishop of Salisbury at the beginning of this chapter (page 119), and answer the question below.

A lazy Prince, no Council, no money, no reputation at home or abroad. It is strange how everybody doth nowadays reflect upon Oliver and commend him, what brave things he did and made all the neighbour princes fear him; while here a prince, come in with all the love and prayers and good liking of his people, hath lost all so soon.

Does the extract from Samuel Pepys support the statements made by the Bishop of Salisbury about Charles II?

James II, 1685–88

During the 1680s, hostility towards James had reduced, and when he became king in 1685, relations with Parliament were cordial. James forgave even those who had tried to have him excluded from the throne. Parliament granted him a generous life income, including all of the proceeds of shipping duties and customs duties. Within just three years, however, he had been overthrown.

The Monmouth Rebellion, 1685

In the spring of 1685, James faced a rebellion from James Scott, the Duke of Monmouth. Monmouth was the eldest illegitimate son of Charles II who claimed to have legal documents proving that he was the legitimate heir to Charles. Importantly for many people, he was a Protestant.

■ The Duke of Monmouth pleading for his life at the feet of James II; a nineteenth-century painting by John Pettie

In June, Monmouth and his supporters landed in Dorset. He had expected to raise a large army but was joined by only about 6000 unemployed labourers and farmworkers. Eventually, Monmouth's army was defeated by the royal army at the Battle of Sedgemoor.

Monmouth was condemned to execution for committing treason against the king, and was beheaded in the Tower of London on 15 July.

Judge Jeffreys and the Bloody Assizes

Following Monmouth's rebellion, James ordered a ruthless clampdown to restore his authority. In the West Country, he relied on Lord Chief Justice Jeffreys, who gained notoriety for the part he played in the Bloody Assizes that followed. The Assizes (sessions of a local court) took place in Winchester, Dorchester and Taunton between August and September 1685, with five judges led by Jeffreys. They dealt with about 2000 prisoners, around 300 of whom were eventually executed. A further 800 or so were transported to the West Indies, reportedly to be sold as slaves.

After Monmouth's Rebellion, James requested a large standing army. Although Parliament had been prepared to grant control of the army to Charles II on the restoration of the monarchy in 1660, it was very unusual to keep a professional army in peacetime. Parliament was also very concerned about James's plans to place Catholics in command of several of the regiments – thus ignoring the Test Act of 1673.

When the previously supportive Parliament objected to these measures, James ordered Parliament to be dissolved in November 1685, and it never met again in his reign.

James and religion

James II was a Catholic and his enemies feared, perhaps rightly, that he wanted to restore England to the Catholic religion. He appointed Catholics as his advisors, judges, university chancellors and officers in the army. He sacked ministers who opposed him. Monasteries were opened and, from 1687, he allowed Catholics to worship openly. A new ecclesiastical court was set up to expel Anglican clergy who criticised the King.

In April 1687, James issued a Declaration of Indulgence (as his brother had in 1672) in an attempt to remove the laws against Catholics. He commanded that his Declaration should be read out in every church in the country. William Sancroft, the Archbishop of Canterbury, and six other bishops refused to do this and were arrested. They were tried but found not guilty.

This was the first time in history that an English king had lost a court case. James's failure to bully the bishops into accepting his religious changes was met with celebration all over England. Bonfires were lit across the country and the tide of popular opinion turned strongly against the King.

The Glorious Revolution

After the release of the seven bishops, leading Whigs and Tories invited William of Orange, the ruler of Holland, to save Protestantism in England and protect the rights of his wife. William was married to Mary, the eldest daughter of James II from his first marriage to the Protestant Anne Hyde. The invitation became more urgent as James's second wife, the Catholic Mary of Modena, had given birth to a son in June 1688, a Catholic, and now heir to the throne (see family tree on page 127).

Rumours spread that this baby, called James Edward Stuart, was not the son of James and Mary of Modena at all. It was said that Mary of Modena had not been pregnant, and that a baby boy had been smuggled into the palace and secretly put into the royal bed in a warming pan (a metal container holding hot coals that was used to warm the bed).

William set sail from the Netherlands with an army of around 15 000 Dutch and English soldiers. On 5 November 1688 (the anniversary of the Gunpowder Plot), he landed at Brixham, in Devon. At the head of his army he marched towards London and was joined on the way by local gentry and men waving orange banners and cheering their 'Protestant saviours'. Perhaps James could have dealt with this threat effectively if he had taken decisive action, but he dithered and the moment was lost. And as the year came to an end, and James II fled to France, another English monarch had lost his throne; this was to be known as the Glorious Revolution.

■ The arrival of William of Orange at Brixham; from a nineteenth-century history book

Exercise 8.7

Read the following sources and answer the questions below.

SOURCE A: From the introduction to a modern historian's account of the Glorious Revolution.

The Glorious Revolution happened because of repeated abuses of power by King James II during his reign from 1685 to 1688. Among these abuses, he suspended acts of Parliament, collected taxes not authorized by law, and undermined the independence of the legal system and the universities. Furthermore, he attempted to impose Catholicism on a Protestant country. In November of 1688 William of Orange and his wife Mary, daughter of James

II, invaded England with the popular support of the English people and much of the English nobility. James ultimately fled for France without significant bloodshed taking place. In January 1689 a Convention assembled in London to determine the succession of the English Crown. After much debate the Convention drafted a Declaration of Rights and offered the throne of England jointly to William and Mary.

SOURCE B: From a modern biography of John Churchill by Emery Walker, published in 2007.

The defeat of the rebels at Sedgemoor was largely due to [Churchill's] coolness, and he was loyal to the new King, James II, until the success of William of Orange's usurpation was inevitable. Churchill was a firm Anglican and when James II's Catholic leanings became obvious, he had open communication with William of Orange; but it is difficult to believe that religion alone would have changed his allegiance.

SOURCE C: From an article by historian Graham Goodlad, published in 2007.

The traditional view of the Glorious Revolution was that it saved England from the power-seeking designs of James II and secured the development of constitutional monarchy, civil and religious liberty and the rule of law.

SOURCE D: From an account of the flight into exile of James II, written at the time.

At Gravesend the King remembered how his own father (Charles I) had been treated. He did not want to agree to William of Orange's demands, nor those of Parliament. He could see that nothing but the Crown would satisfy his son-in-law (William of Orange).

1 What can you learn from Source A about the reasons behind the Glorious Revolution?

2 What can you learn from Source B about the personality of John Churchill?

3 How far do Sources A and C agree on the faults of James II?

4 Using all the sources and your own knowledge, how far do you agree with the view that it was the desertion of men like John Churchill that lead to James II being replaced as king by William of Orange?

Exercise 8.8

1 If you had been an advisor to James II in 1685, what advice would you have given him? Write a few sentences.

2 Explain why James II can be considered an unsuccessful king.

Science and the arts

Before we see how William and Mary fared, we should stop to look at what sort of country they had arrived in. We have already seen how Henry VIII relied on the services of a portrait painter when choosing one of his wives, and Elizabeth used painters to build her image as 'the Virgin Queen'. Under the Tudors, architects were employed to build grand palaces and music flourished. Then came the time of Cromwell and the Puritan period of austerity, to be followed by the reign of Charles II, the 'merrie monarch'.

Artists

Hans Holbein

Hans Holbein (c.1497–1543) lived in England between 1526 and 1543 and his paintings are some of the most familiar images from the Tudor age, particularly from the reign of Henry VIII. It was Holbein who 'misled' Henry into believing that Anne of Cleves was attractive!

Nicholas Hilliard

Nicholas Hilliard (c.1547–1619) was an English painter who, rather than producing the huge paintings that were so popular at this time, produced what we call miniatures, tiny paintings of men and women, over 200 of which survive. Although originally head and shoulder pictures, Hilliard went on to paint full-length portraits, in exquisite detail, but still in miniature.

Anthony van Dyck

For the reign of Charles I, much of our knowledge of what people looked like and what they wore comes from the work of Anthony van Dyck (1599–1641). Van Dyck painted many portraits of Charles and his wife, along with other members of the aristocracy.

You can find out all about the great artists and writers who worked during these years by looking in your library, visiting museums or using the internet. Below are listed some of the people you might like to research.

■ The Earl of Cumberland; a miniature painted c.1590 by Nicholas Hilliard

■ The five children of Charles I; from a painting produced in 1637 by van Dyck. The children are, left to right, Mary, James, Charles, Elizabeth and Anne.

Writers

You have already read about William Shakespeare in Chapter 6, and he was certainly the most influential writer of the period. During the reigns of Elizabeth and James I, England produced a large number of poets and playwrights, many of whom influenced the great English poets of the nineteenth and early twentieth centuries.

Edmund Spenser

Edmund Spenser (1552–99) is regarded as one of the forefathers of English poetry, and was a great favourite of Elizabeth I. His most famous poem is *The Faerie Queene*, an allegory in praise of Elizabeth. It is thought that Shakespeare attended his funeral.

Christopher Marlowe

Christopher Marlowe (1564–93) was a playwright, popular with great men such as Sir Walter Raleigh, and famous for having written the first notable English play in blank verse. There are some who think that Marlowe was responsible for writing some of Shakespeare's early plays. He died after a fight in a tavern!

John Bunyan

John Bunyan (1628–88) was a non-conformist preacher who was thrown into prison for preaching without a licence. He is best remembered for his famous allegorical work, *The Pilgrim's Progress*, which tells the story of Christian and his willingness to give up his family and home in order to find salvation.

Developments in science and medicine

Before 1500, scientific knowledge was based on the ideas of the ancient Greeks. In the sixteenth century, these ideas came to be challenged. Probably the most famous example of this was the insistence by the Polish astronomer Copernicus that the Earth travelled around the Sun, rather than vice versa. The work of such men sparked a movement which came to be called the Enlightenment, and many of its leading scholars lived and worked in England during this period.

Francis Bacon

Francis Bacon (1561–1626) was Lord Chancellor under James I and is seen as one of the fathers of modern science. Bacon challenged the old belief that scientific knowledge could be gained by discussion, holding instead that it was obtained by observation, the so-called empirical method.

William Harvey

William Harvey (1578–1657) was physician (doctor) to James I and Charles I, and is famous for having accurately shown how blood is pumped around the body by the heart. Not everyone valued his work, however, as this diary entry from one of his friends shows:

I have heard him say, that after his book of the Circulation of the Blood came out, he fell mightily in his practice, losing many patients, and 'twas believed he was crack-brained.

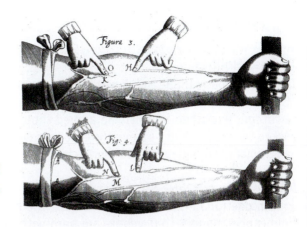

■ One of William Harvey's drawings from his book produced in 1628

◯ The Royal Society

Charles II gave his support to the work of scientists such as Harvey and in 1660 he encouraged the setting up of the Royal Society to promote the work of English scientists. This royal support allowed them to continue their work without fear of attack; for much of what they were working on undermined some of the teachings of the Church.

Some famous members of the Royal Society during the late seventeenth century were:

- Robert Boyle (1627–91); a scientist who studied the behaviour of gases
- Sir Christopher Wren (1632–1723); an architect who redesigned St Paul's Cathedral
- Robert Hooke (1635–1703); a scientist who popularised the use of the microscope
- Sir Isaac Newton (1642–1727); a scientist who studied gravity and the laws of motion
- Edmond Halley (1656–1742); an astronomer who discovered Halley's Comet.

All of these men and more had an important impact on our understanding of the world around us. And yet they realised that, the more they learnt, the more they needed to know. As Newton said towards the end of his life:

I do not know what I may appear to the world, but to myself I seem only to have been a boy playing on the seashore, while the great ocean of truth lay all undiscovered before me.

■ Sir Isaac Newton and Edmond Halley; twentieth-century engraving by Patrick Nicolle

Philosophers

Thomas Hobbes

Thomas Hobbes (1588–1679) was a keen royalist who spent most of the interregnum in exile in France. In his most famous book, *Leviathan*, published in 1651, he argued that people are, from birth, wicked by nature, and not therefore fit to govern. The best form of government, he believed, was monarchy.

John Locke

John Locke (1632–1704) believed almost the exact opposite to Hobbes. He thought that people are born without any innate ideas, and that they should form their own opinions through the use of reason, rather than meekly accepting the word of those in authority over them. He was strongly opposed to the concept of a hereditary monarchy.

Exercise 8.9

1 Find out what you can about the artists, writers, scientists and philosophers mentioned in this chapter. Create an illustrated brochure, divided into sections, in which you describe their life and work.

2 Find out what you can about the advances in science and learning in the seventeenth century, using the internet and the resources in your library. Explain why it is useful for historians to study the history of science and learning, as well as the history of wars and politics.

3 Explain what we learn about the history of this period by looking at the life of one artist.

4 Considering the work of Sir Christopher Wren, explain why it is useful for historians to study the history of buildings during this period.

5 Explain why you think portraits are useful to people studying sixteenth- and seventeenth-century England.

9 William and Mary, and Anne

William and Mary, 1689–1702

Following the Glorious Revolution, William and Mary became joint monarchs. The Crown passed to Mary because she was the eldest daughter of James II by his first wife (see family tree on page 163); but real power was set to pass to her husband, William of Orange, the ruler of Holland. Indeed, William threatened to return to Holland unless the English Parliament made him king, and on 11 April 1689 they were crowned King William III and Queen Mary II.

This was not without conditions, however. William and Mary signed a Bill of Rights under which:

- the Crown could only be inherited by a Protestant
- Parliament should meet frequently and MPs should have freedom of speech
- no taxes could be imposed without the agreement of Parliament
- the King could not have a standing army during peacetime.

■ William III and Mary II; an etching by Romeyn de Hooghe, c.1689

On the religious front, the Toleration Act of 1689 allowed Puritans and 'dissenters' to worship as they wished and freedom of worship was given to everyone who accepted most of the beliefs of the Anglican Church.

Catholics and extreme Protestants, however, were still barred from holding public office. And it was in 1688 that the following inscription was added to the base of the monument set up near the outbreak of the Fire of London:

Here by permission of heaven, hell broke loose upon this Protestant city ... The most dreadful Burning of this City; begun and carried on by the treachery and malice of the Popish faction ... Popish frenzy which wrought such horrors, is not yet quenched ...

○ James II in Ireland

When William of Orange had arrived in England, and James II had seen his support disappear, James had fled to France. There, the Catholic King, Louis XIV, had helped him to raise an army and James then sailed to Ireland, where he was welcomed by the largely Catholic population. James seized control of Dublin and then marched north to Ulster, where he besieged the city of Derry, where the Protestants had taken refuge. The siege of Derry lasted three and a half months, and thousands of Protestants died, but eventually William III's army managed to relieve the siege by breaking through the Catholic defences in the harbour.

William himself then sailed to Ireland to deal with James, once and for all, and defeated him at the Battle of the Boyne on 12 July 1690. James fled back to France and William took control of Ireland once more.

> The date of the Battle of the Boyne, known simply as 'The Twelfth', is celebrated by Protestant 'Orangemen' with ceremonial marches, particularly in Northern Ireland. Why do you think these continue to cause tension and resentment between Protestant and Catholic communities?

The struggle against France

The King of France was bitterly opposed to William III and had supported James II in his efforts to reclaim his throne. After Mary died in 1694, William devoted all his efforts to war with France, with some success. An Anglo-Dutch navy defeated the French at the Battles of Barfleur and La Hogue, and then went to the aid of Barcelona, which was under attack from the French, thereby increasing Spain's resistance to the French. Eventually, Louis XIV made peace with William in 1697.

○ Relations with Parliament

Parliament was determined not to allow a monarch to rule unchecked, the way the early Stuart kings had, and in 1694 the Triennial Act laid down that Parliament was to be called at least once every three years. A grant of money was made to the monarchy, called the Civil List, and any sums of money beyond that had to be agreed by Parliament. The royal accounts were to be scrutinised by Parliament.

Command of the army and navy, and the right to choose ministers and to decide foreign policy, remained with the Crown. But, in effect, the absolute power that Charles I and Charles II had claimed was theirs by right, based on the Divine Right of Kings, was being replaced by a partnership between Parliament and the Crown. This partnership was the basis of the constitutional monarchy which survives to this day, under which the monarch rules but is bound by a set of rules imposed on him or her by Parliament.

◯ The Act of Settlement, 1701

Perhaps more controversially, Parliament claimed the right to decide the succession. William and Mary had no children, so the question of the succession had to be decided; Mary's half-brother, James Edward Stuart, was her closest male relation, but he was a Catholic, so Parliament decreed that the throne should pass to Mary's younger sister, Anne.

Anne was married to Prince George of Denmark and, despite seventeen pregnancies, had failed to produce any children who survived into adulthood. The question of who would become monarch after Anne thus also had to be decided.

The Act of Settlement decreed that the descendants of James II and Mary of Modena would be forever barred from the Crown. After the death of Anne, the succession was to pass to James I's granddaughter Sophia of Hanover. The Act of Settlement thus led to what we know as the Hanoverian succession.

Exercise 9.1

1 Make two lists, one for 'Crown' and one for 'Parliament', showing what each side gained in the first few years of the reign of William and Mary.

2 Which was the more powerful by the end of William's reign: Crown or Parliament? Give at least two reasons for your answer.

3 Explain why the Glorious Revolution is an important event in the history of English and British government.

◯ Anne, 1702–14

William III died in 1702 and was succeeded by Mary's younger sister, Anne. When Anne came to the throne, the question of the succession had been settled in favour of the Hanoverian dynasty, but this was not accepted by all. In particular, it was far from popular in Scotland.

When James I had become King of England in 1603, Scotland had continued to have its own Parliament and government. The two countries were separate, and England was always much richer than its northern neighbour. As England's empire began to develop over this period, largely on the back of growing trade and the activities of companies such as the English East India Company, Scotland felt cut off from this success, and its merchants were banned from trading freely with England's colonies.

So, with relations between the two countries far from cordial, it was perhaps not surprising that Scotland should insist on its freedom to choose its own monarch, nor that it should decide that the very man excluded from the English throne should become the next King of Scotland: James Edward Stuart, the son of James II and Mary of Modena.

Furthermore, Scotland was keen to make clear that it did not support the English when England declared war on France in 1702. With relations with Scotland deteriorating, the danger of a Franco-Scottish alliance was very real. It therefore became something of a priority for Anne's government to sort out the relationship between England and Scotland.

■ The Articles of Union 1707

The Act of Union, 1707

Some (mainly English) MPs were keen to unite the English and Scottish Parliaments, so that they could debate on the issue together. Others, particularly the Scots, were less keen. While the debate continued, the English Parliament voted a grant of money to be paid to those Scottish merchants who had lost money in English companies trading abroad, and this helped to bring the Scots round. In 1707, after months of bitter wrangling, both in London and Edinburgh, the Parliaments of the two countries were united and the Union between England and Scotland was brought into effect, represented by the flag of the kingdom of Great Britain.

Under the Union, Scotland would send 45 MPs to the House of Commons in London, and sixteen peers to the House of Lords. Scotland would keep its own established Church, but everything else – coinage, taxation, army, trade, flag and Parliament – would be shared jointly with England.

■ The 'Old' Union Flag, used after 1707

Exercise 9.2

1 Explain why the Act of Union of 1707 was an important event in the political history of Britain.

Marlborough and the war against France

In 1702, England had declared war against France. France had been waging a war on Spain, in which we have already seen the Anglo-Dutch navy intervened in the 1690s at Barcelona. Charles II, the childless King of Spain, died in 1699 and left his throne to Philip of Anjou. He was the grandson of Louis XIV, the King of France, whose ambition had always been to expand his kingdom. Louis not only claimed Spain but also threatened the Netherlands and Austria. England declared war on France and persuaded other European nations to join her in a Grand Alliance. The war that followed is called the War of Spanish Succession. Austria, Prussia, Denmark and

The Union of England and Scotland has lasted until the present day, and it was only in 1998 that the Scottish Parliament, disbanded in 1707, was re-established. Find out what you can about this process, which is called 'devolution'.

Holland all joined the Grand Alliance, whose principal aim was to prevent the creation of a united France and Spain.

The Blenheim campaign

At the beginning of the war, the opposing forces faced each other in the Low Countries (the area of north-west Europe which today contains Belgium, the Netherlands and Luxembourg). In 1703–04, the French moved into Germany and Italy where they inflicted a heavy defeat on the Austrian forces, threatening to take Vienna and thus force Austria out of the war.

■ The Duke of Marlborough leading the charge at the Battle of Blenheim; painting by John Wootton, c.1743

The leader of England's forces was John Churchill, the Duke of Marlborough. Marlborough was determined to assist the Austrians, and so marched his army across Europe. He joined up with the Germans, whose army was led by Prince Eugene of Savoy, thus creating an allied army of 56 000 men. By the time that the allies met up with the French forces, Marlborough's army had covered almost 300 miles. Of this movement, one of his aides said:

Surely never was such a march carried on with more order and regularity, and with less fatigue to both man and horse.

The forces of Marlborough and Prince Eugene took the town of Donauwörth in early July, securing their crossing of the Danube River. Marlborough then began to destroy many local villages, trying to provoke the Elector of Bavaria into fighting him. Meanwhile, Louis XIV had sent a French army, under the command of Marshal Tallard, to reinforce the French and Bavarian forces and defeat the allied army.

Armies of the Blenheim campaign

Marshal Tallard was supremely confident of his army, as the French had remained virtually unbeaten for 50 years. The infantry of every nation was equipped with flintlock muskets, which could be loaded and fired much more quickly than the older matchlocks. Pikes were no longer needed because of the invention of the bayonet, a blade that could be attached to the end of a musket. French infantry fired in mass volleys and stood five lines deep in their fighting formation. The Dutch and English stood in three lines and fired in smaller groups, or platoons, meaning they

■ British infantrymen at the Battle of Blenheim

produced a constant running fire. Each side wore a long coat over a waistcoat with large cuffs, with the collar coloured to show the different regiments. French troops tended to wear white coats and the British red. The tricorn or three-cornered hat was worn by both sides.

Horsemen no longer wore a lot of armour, but instead had coats and tricorn hats. The French cavalry were trained to advance and fire their guns at the enemy before charging. English cavalry advanced at a quick trot and went straight in with their swords. The artillery was slow and cumbersome to move, but could dominate areas of the battlefield if grouped in large enough numbers. At long range, the cannons fired solid shot. At close range, they fired clusters of smaller balls called grapeshot.

The Battle of Blenheim, 13 August 1704

Once Marshal Tallard had joined his army with that of the Elector of Bavaria he advanced across the Danube River to threaten the smaller allied army. He fully expected Marlborough and Prince Eugene to retreat to protect their supply line, and Marlborough encouraged his enemies to believe this. Marching his force in nine great columns, Marlborough moved west – under the very noses of the Franco-Bavarian armies – but instead of retreating, he lined up for battle. His full force was not completely organised until 1 p.m., as the right flank under Prince Eugene had further to march, but English troops under Lord Cutts had already opened the battle at noon by attacking the village of Blenheim (see diagram on page 143).

The Franco-Bavarian forces had established a strong position, with their right flank stretching from the Danube west through the villages of Blenheim, Oberklau and Lutzingen. The Elector of Bavaria, along with French forces commanded by Marshal Marsin, held the line to the left, while Marshal Tallard's army held the centre and right. Running in front of the whole Franco-Bavarian line was a marshy stream called the Nebel, which the allied troops would have to cross as they attacked. Tallard was confident that if the enemy did try to cross, his cavalry would destroy them. He therefore put his troops some distance to the south of the stream. Marsin and the Elector, who had fought the allied forces before, put their defensive line at the edge of the Nebel.

Marlborough's plan was daring as he was attacking a force much larger than his own. But he knew that he had an advantage in cavalry and intended to use it. In the large open plain between Blenheim and Oberklau, Tallard had placed a large force of cavalry, with a much smaller force of infantry in support. This is where Marlborough spotted the enemy's weak spot. He thus planned to attack both flanks of the Franco-Bavarian armies and keep them busy, so that when he launched a grand attack in the centre no forces would be able to reinforce the outnumbered French troops there. This would only work if all of Marlborough's commanders understood their missions and worked together.

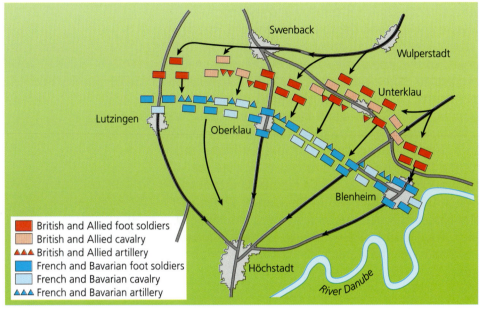

Legend:
- ■ British and Allied foot soldiers
- ■ British and Allied cavalry
- ▲▲▲ British and Allied artillery
- ■ French and Bavarian foot soldiers
- ■ French and Bavarian cavalry
- ▲▲▲ French and Bavarian artillery

■ The Battle of Blenheim, 13 August 1704

Lord Cutts' attacks on Blenheim were fiercely fought but successful. As the Marquis de Mérode-Westerloo, a cavalry commander under Marshal Tallard, reported:

> *... the English infantry ... at last attacked the village of Blenheim, shortly after midday ... The first volleys in this attack had hardly been fired when the two lines of our infantry, some twenty-seven battalions in all, whose orders I believe had been to support the position, entered the village most prematurely and ill-advisedly ... The men were so crowded in upon one another that they could not even fire, let alone receive or carry out any orders ...*

Meanwhile, Prince Eugene on the right flank faced a much more daunting task. His forces were bombarded with artillery fire as they struggled over the Nebel. Nonetheless his infantry and cavalry carried out a series of attacks upon Lutzingen which, while ultimately unsuccessful in gaining ground, kept the Franco-Bavarian forces on the left fully focused on his force.

Marlborough's forces crossed the Nebel in the centre of the battlefield, and reached firmer ground. As the Marquis de Mérode-Westerloo recalled:

> *The enemy began to cross the marsh which we had considered impassable, leading their horses by the bridles. So they were allowed to get over and remount right in front of our positions.*

Marlborough's brother Charles Churchill commanded the infantry, and the Prince of Hesse commanded the cavalry. When the French cavalry began to attack, they failed to come as one large force, but in many small charges, so that the plain was full of charging and counter-charging horsemen. When the French finally sent in a major cavalry charge, the infantry greeted them with volleys of musket fire that sent them tumbling back. So the allied forces advanced, using a combination of cavalry charge, infantry volleys and cannon fire to push back the French. Marshal Tallard could not find reinforcements from either flank of the Franco-Bavarian forces, as they were too busy with the allied attacks upon them. When Charles Churchill's forces broke the French infantry stationed in the centre, a second line of allied cavalry passed through the infantry lines and charged the weakened French. The French cavalry, despite the best efforts of Marshal Tallard, broke and ran. The Marquis de Mérode-Westerloo was caught up in the rout:

> *We soon found ourselves faced by numerous enemy squadrons on no less than three sides – and we were borne back on top of one another. So tight was the press that my horse was carried along some three hundred paces without putting hoof to ground, right to the edge of a deep ravine: down we plunged a good twenty feet into a swampy meadow ...*

Mérode-Westerloo was lucky to survive; many of the French cavalry drowned in the Danube.

By seven o'clock it was clear that Marshal Tallard's army had been virtually destroyed. The Elector of Bavaria managed to withdraw, and Prince Eugene's troops were too exhausted to follow. Blenheim was surrounded by allied infantry, and the 27 battalions of French infantry that were caught in the village surrendered. Marshal Tallard also gave himself up. Captain Robert Parker, an English officer, reckoned that:

> *The loss of the enemy was computed to be at least 40,000 killed, drowned and taken ... The loss on our side also was great, we had near 6,000 killed, and above 8,000 wounded.*

The consequences of Blenheim

In one great battle, in which over 100 000 men fought, the Duke of Marlborough had completely changed the course of the War of Spanish Succession. From being the aggressor, the French were now on the defensive, fighting to defend their borders. Vienna was saved and Austria remained in the Grand Alliance, while the Elector of Bavaria lost control of his territory. All this was achieved by a man who, at the age of 54, had never commanded a major army in battle.

Further victories for Marlborough followed at Ramillies (1706), Oudenarde (1708) and Malplaquet (1709), and by 1714 France was defeated. At the Peace of Utrecht a series of treaties between France and the countries of Europe were signed, bringing the war to an end. France agreed to recognise Anne as the rightful Queen of England, and promised to stop supporting the rival claims of James Edward Stuart. France also conceded territories to England in the New World, including Newfoundland, Nova Scotia, the Hudson Bay territory and the island of St Kitts. The threatened unification of the thrones of France and Spain was prevented. France had been well and truly beaten, and Marlborough had become a national hero. To reward Marlborough, Queen Anne gave him the royal manor of Woodstock, just north of Oxford, and the promise of a fine palace. That palace, Blenheim Palace, designed by Sir John Vanbrugh, was built between 1705 and 1722 and stands today as a lasting monument to a great victory.

Exercise 9.3

1 Find out what you can about Marlborough's military victories in the war with France. Write a series of newspaper articles, describing the progress of the war, ending with the Treaty of Utrecht.

2 Choose one of Marlborough's victories at Blenheim, Ramillies, Oudenarde or Malplaquet. Explain why Marlborough's forces won this battle.

3 Look at the painting of Marlborough leading England's forces at Blenheim on page 141. How useful is this source as evidence about:

   (a) the Duke of Marlborough

   (b) the Battle of Blenheim?

4 Imagine you are a soldier, fighting with Marlborough in the Blenheim campaign. Write a series of diary entries describing your experiences. Use as much detail from this chapter as you can.

George I and George II

George I, 1714–27

Queen Anne, the last Stuart monarch, died in 1714. The Crown of Great Britain passed by the 1701 Act of Settlement (see page 139) to the House of Hanover. Sophia of Hanover had been named as Anne's heir, but died shortly before Anne and so the throne passed to her son George (see family tree on page 163).

George I was not a popular successor to Anne. He spoke little English and had an awkward manner.

Below is an entry from the diary of Lord Hervey, who knew King George personally:

In truth, he hated the English, looked upon them as King-killers and republicans, grudged them their riches as well as their liberty, thought them overpaid, and said to Lady Sandon one day that he was forced to distribute his favour to people for being rascals and pay them not to cut his throat.

The 1715 Jacobite Rebellion

Almost as soon as he became king, George faced a rebellion from those who opposed the Hanoverian succession. In Parliament, the Whigs supported George, largely because he was not a Catholic, but there were many who wanted the Stuart dynasty to retain the throne, and these people looked to 'the Old Pretender' James Edward Stuart, the son of James II and Mary of Modena. They were known as Jacobites, from *Jacobus*, the Latin for James.

In 1715, the Earl of Mar proclaimed James king. Mar had been secretary of state for Scotland under Anne, but was dismissed from the post by George. He raised a force of between 10 000 and 12 000 men, and at the same time risings in Wales and south-west England occurred. In the north of England a Jacobite force was defeated at the Battle of Preston on 13 November 1715.

■ George I; eighteenth-century portrait by the German artist Godfrey Kneller

The Earl of Mar met government forces led by the Duke of Argyll at the Battle of Sheriffmuir in Perthshire. The battle was inconclusive, and despite the arrival in Scotland of 'the Old Pretender' himself, Mar was unable to break out of the Scottish Highlands and carry his rebellion south into England. In February 1716 James Edward Stuart returned to France and the Jacobite rebellion collapsed. An effort was made to revive it in 1719, with assistance from Spain, but this failed.

After the 1715 rebellion, the British government decided to install a series of army garrisons in Scotland to meet any future threat. These were Fort William, Fort Augustus and Fort George, all of which were linked by a series of roads to the south. The Highlands remained a troublesome area and a special regiment, the Black Watch, was raised under General George Wade to patrol the region and maintain the peace. However, outside the Highlands, Jacobitism declined and most people came to accept the Hanoverian monarchs.

Exercise 10.1

1 Why was King George disliked by some people in Britain? Make a list to show the reasons.

2 Explain why the Jacobite Rebellion of 1715 was a failure.

Parliamentary government

George I had seen off the Jacobite threat but his interests in his own lands in Hanover meant that he was unable to devote as much time to the government of his kingdom as he might have wished. He spent about one-fifth of his time away from England, and when he was absent he placed affairs in the hands of a Regency Council. This council met in a room called the Cabinet, where previously both William III and Anne had attended regular briefing meetings with their ministers, and it is from this room that our modern Cabinet takes its name.

During George's reign, the two parliamentary factions, the Whigs and the Tories, continued to develop. Viscount Bolingbroke, a supporter of James Edward Stuart's claim to the throne, wrote the following about political parties in the early eighteenth century:

We looked upon the Revolution of 1688 to be against our true interest ... to have weakened Church and State. We supposed the Tory Party to be the bulk of the landed interest (landowners and farmers) ... We supposed the Whigs to be so weak a party as to lean for support on the Presbyterians, the Bank of England, on the Dutch and other allies.

George was suspicious of the Tories, for having opposed the Act of Settlement and for their sympathy for the Jacobite risings, and came to depend for his support on the Whigs. After the election in 1715, the Whigs held a majority in the House of Commons, and sought to strengthen their control on power by passing the Septennial Act, requiring the king to call a new Parliament only every seven years (before it had been every three years). Also during this time George I gave up attending Cabinet meetings, and the constitutional monarchy which had been envisaged by the champions of the Glorious Revolution in 1688 was now firmly established.

Sir Robert Walpole

In the absence of the King, a leading Cabinet minister chaired the Cabinet meetings and later reported to the King. Sir Robert Walpole was the leading minister from 1721 to 1742, and is now viewed as having been Britain's first prime minister, although the title was not used officially at the time.

Walpole became the leading minister at a time of financial crisis in Britain. Britain had endured a long period of expensive European wars and was heavily in debt. In Chapter 5 we learnt about joint stock companies and one of those, the South Sea Company, had been granted a valuable monopoly for trading in the South Seas in exchange for its taking on responsibility for this national debt, but the company got into difficulties. Hundreds of investors had been tempted to buy shares in the South Sea Company, encouraged by the exaggerated stories of the opportunities available to the company, and in 1720, what became known as the 'South Sea Bubble' burst. Shares in the company plunged in value, leading to a major crash in the financial markets. A committee was set up to investigate the disaster, and several MPs were found to have been guilty of corruption and were put in prison.

Then, in 1722, there was another Jacobite conspiracy. A leading Tory, Francis Atterbury, the Bishop of Rochester, was involved. Walpole took the opportunity to brand all Tories as Jacobites – with the result that they did not take office again until 1770.

By the time of King George's death in 1727, Walpole and his Cabinet were able to control most of the important parts of government and the Whig party was firmly in control of power.

■ Sir Robert Walpole; eighteenth-century portrait by Jean Baptiste Van Loc

The rise of a colonial empire

■ Britain's Empire at the time of George I

By the end of the reign of George I in 1727, Britain owned territory in America, the West Indies and parts of Canada, as well as having trading bases in India and the important colony of Gibraltar, near Spain.

In America, the colonies had been started by a range of different people, from those who left England on religious grounds like the Puritans, to adventurers who were simply seeking their fortune. As the American colonies grew they developed as useful markets for British-made goods and the source of raw materials. The traders in America and the West Indies eventually began to buy slaves from Africa to work on the plantations and found that vast profits were to be made. What became known as the Triangular Trade developed, whereby British traders took manufactured goods to Africa and exchanged them for slaves. The slaves were then taken to America to be sold to plantation owners and the produce from the plantations was then brought to Britain through the ports of Bristol and Liverpool. But the true centre of the colonial empire's trade was the City of London, with goods from all over the world passing through its docks and warehouses.

As we have seen, various British trading companies were founded at the time of the Stuarts and they traded all over the known world. Many of these became extremely wealthy and gained much political influence. The most important ones were the Virginia Company, the Hudson Bay Company, the Royal African Company, the East India Company, the Eastland Company and the Levant Company.

There are many more examples of British trading companies that were set up at this time. Which ones are still operating today?

Sugar
Tobacco
Cotton
Coffee
to Europe

Alcohol
Horses
Guns
Pots
to Africa

Slaves
to the Americas

■ Goods to Africa

■ Slaves to the West
Indies

■ Produce to Europe   ■ The Triangular Trade

Exercise 10.2

1 Write a sentence or two to explain the meaning of the following terms:

(a) Parliament

(b) Cabinet

(c) Septennial Act

(d) South Sea Bubble

2 Explain how the rise of the colonial empire affected Britain.

3 Explain the reasons why Robert Walpole has come to be seen as Britain's first prime minister.

4 Select three of the trading companies listed above and find out more information on each one. Write a prospectus in which you try to persuade people to buy shares in the companies.

George II, 1727–60

George II became king in 1727 and was to rule for 33 years. Although like his father he preferred Hanover to Britain, he could speak good English and took an interest in British government.

■ George II at the Battle of Dettingen with the Duke of Cumberland; c.1743 by John Wootton

◯ The War of Jenkins' Ear, 1739–42

One thing that George II was not prepared to accept was the bullying tactics of the Spanish. The Spanish had imposed severe limitations on British merchants trading with the Spanish colonies of South America. The 1729 Treaty of Seville gave the Spanish the right to board British vessels in Spanish waters, and the British very much resented this.

In 1731, a British ship, the *Rebecca*, was found smuggling goods into the Spanish colonies. Spanish sailors boarded the ship and a fight broke out, during which the captain of the British ship, Robert Jenkins, had one of his ears cut off.

The incident sparked a major row, especially when Jenkins displayed the mutilated ear in Parliament on his return to England. War on Spain was declared and, in 1739, things began well when the British captured Porto Bello in Spanish Panama. At a dinner held to celebrate this victory, the song 'God Save the King' was sung for the first time.

However, events then turned against the British. Four expeditions against Spanish strongholds in 1740–42 were disasters and the British were forced to give up any hope of achieving their aim of dominating trade with the Spanish colonies of South America. It had been a humiliating failure, and in 1742 Sir Robert Walpole, George II's chief minister, resigned.

◯ Britain and the War of the Austrian Succession, 1742–48

No sooner had the war with Spain come to an end than war with France broke out. In 1742 there was a dispute between Prussia and Austria over the succession to the Austrian throne following the death of the Emperor, Charles VI, in 1740. Charles had left the throne to his daughter, Maria Theresa, whose claim was challenged by the newly crowned Frederick of Prussia, supported by France.

Britain became involved in 1742, at which point the war also became known as King George's War, because the French threatened to invade Hanover, of which George II was ruler. A combined Anglo-Hanoverian army, under the personal command of George II, defeated the French at Dettingen on 27 June 1743.

The Anglo-French conflict also extended to the colonies in America. In 1745, French forces raided the British fortifications in Maine, while Fort Louisburg, a powerful French stronghold on Cape Breton Island in Nova Scotia, was captured by New Englanders supported by an English fleet.

The war was ended in 1748 by the Treaty of Aix-la-Chapelle. The British returned Fort Louisburg to the French, but regained trading rights to Spanish America.

The 1745 Jacobite Rebellion

Meanwhile, back at home, many Catholics, particularly Scottish Catholics from the Highlands, continued to believe that James Edward Stuart (the son of James II, known as the 'warming-pan baby', see page 131) was the rightful king of Scotland and England. James was now living in Italy where he had been given a home by the Pope, and in 1720 he had a son, Charles, who was to become known as Bonnie Prince Charlie.

In 1744, Louis XV of France offered to finance an invasion of England with the aim of putting James on the throne. James had been involved in a number of failed rebellions and, at the age of 57, was not too enthusiastic. A French fleet was smashed in a storm before reaching England, but James's son Charles was keen, and in July 1745 he landed on an island on the west coast of Scotland with a small band of men, hoping to unite Scotland behind him.

In August, with a force of about 200 men, Bonnie Prince Charlie raised his standard at Glenfinnan, and before long had recruited support from the Camerons, Mackintoshes and Frasers, increasing the size of his army to over 4000. These men were Highlander Scots, who lived in the wilds of northern Scotland and were raised from childhood to fight. John Hume, captured by Jacobite Highlanders in 1746, wrote that:

... they always appeared like warriors; as if their weapons had been limbs and members of their bodies: they were never seen without them; they travelled, they attended fairs and markets, nay they went to church with their broadswords and dirks [long daggers]; and in latter times with their muskets and pistols.

> The clan system was extremely important in Scotland because it determined loyalties in times of conflict. Find out what you can about it. If you have Scottish ancestry, which clan do you belong to?

Fiercely loyal to their clan chiefs and showing their individual bravery, the Highlanders were not disciplined troops. In the right circumstances, however, the 'Highland Charge' was terrifying for those facing it. After first firing their muskets, the Highlanders would fling them to the ground, throw off the plaid that they wore around their waist and shoulders, pull out their broadswords and – holding a small shield in the other hand – rush headlong at their enemy. Only well-trained veteran troops had much chance of stopping this charge.

On 16 September, the Jacobite army captured Edinburgh and five days later defeated a Government army under General Cope at the Battle of Prestonpans, east of the city. One of the Jacobites described the battle:

Key

→ Bonnie Prince Charlie and the Jacobite forces

⇢ The Duke of Cumberland and the government forces

■ The Jacobite Rebellion, 1745

We rushed in with such fury upon the enemy that they did not have time to reload. Arms and legs were cut off and heads split to the shoulders, never such wounds were seen. The enemy were chased so closely that they threw away their standards and colours and abandoned their horses. Eighty-four officers and fourteen hundred others were taken prisoner.

However, despite this early success, support for Charles was limited, and when he marched south into England, very few joined him and indeed some of his Highland troops returned across the border.

Undeterred, Charles continued south and on 4 December the Jacobites reached Derby, only 125 miles from London. George II was so worried about the threat posed by Charles that he was preparing to leave London and had recalled large numbers of troops from Europe to fight the Jacobites. However, Prince Charles's commanders, too, were worried as they knew large Government forces were gathering and they convinced the reluctant Prince Charles to return to Scotland.

On reaching Scotland, the Jacobites were reinforced by more clansmen and a force of 750 Irish troops sent from France. Charles turned his attention to taking Stirling Castle using cannons sent from France, but a Government force under General Hawley attacked him on 17 January 1746. The Battle of Falkirk was fought in the driving rain, which favoured the Highlanders and their charge. Hawley's 8000 men were defeated and retreated back to Edinburgh.

The Battle of Culloden, 16 April 1746

A rather nervous George II had recalled his third son, William, Duke of Cumberland, who had been fighting in Europe, to deal with the Jacobite rebels. Cumberland reorganised the battered Government forces in Edinburgh and then began to advance north while the Jacobite army fell back to Inverness. In April, the Duke of Cumberland and his army caught up with the Jacobites at Culloden Moor, a few miles from Inverness. This was not the battlefield of choice for the Jacobites' most competent commander, Lord George Murray, as he realised that the open moorland was a good place for the Duke of Cumberland to use his superior artillery and cavalry. Murray urged Prince Charles to withdraw but unfortunately Prince Charles failed to listen to this good advice. Instead, he ordered a night attack on the Government army's position eight miles away on 15 April. Food supplies were running low for the Jacobites, so many of them were out in the countryside looking for food rather than joining in the planned attack. The plan was a disaster and Prince Charles was forced to turn the men back to Culloden Moor.

The Duke of Cumberland had his well-fed and organised army on the march before dawn on 16 April, planning to catch the Jacobites unprepared. In this he succeeded as the exhausted Jacobites had

had no time to rest or to gather the many men still looking for food. Of Prince Charles's army of 7000 men, at first only 1000 were actually ready to fight. The Prince was urged to retreat to Inverness to regroup, but he refused. When Lord Murray was asked what he thought he replied 'We are putting an end to a bad affair.' By the time Cumberland's army was drawn up for battle, the Jacobites would have 5000 men to face a Government army of 9000.

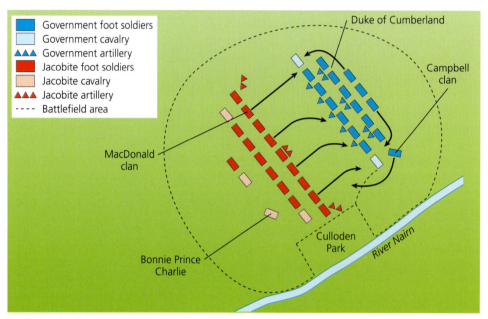

■ The Battle of Culloden, 16 April 1746

Cumberland's red-coated army was placed in two lines of regiments with cavalry on each flank. Units of Campbells – a loyal Scottish clan – were sent to the left, using stonewalls for protection.

The Jacobites lined up also in two main lines, with mostly Highlanders in the front. To the anger of the MacDonald clan, who claimed they should have the honour of being on the right of the line, they were instead placed on the left. Behind the second line were what was left of the Jacobite cavalry, many without horses and so fighting on foot.

At one o'clock, with rain falling, the Jacobites opened fire with their artillery, to little effect, although one ball did pass close to the Duke of Cumberland on his large grey horse. He had celebrated his 25th birthday only the day before. The Government army's more accurate guns replied and began to cause casualties among the ranks of the Jacobite army – including cutting a man in two just metres from where Prince Charles stood. Charles retired further back and thus lost any real control of the battle.

After 25 minutes of standing in position and suffering mounting losses, Lord Murray's own brigade of Highlanders on the right flank had had enough. As the Government's artillery began to fire with grapeshot (groups of iron balls that fanned out as they left the cannon barrel) the Highlanders of the right flank charged into the rain and smoke towards the hated redcoats. Soon afterwards the middle of the Jacobite front line also charged, crying out their battle cry of 'Claymore!' and running into a wall of bullets and grapeshot. One British officer reported:

the King's men discharged a complete running fire that dropped [the Scots] down as they came on.

The Brown Bess muskets used by the Government troops could be loaded and discharged up to five times a minute, and were being fired in mass volleys by the lines of red-coated soldiers.

The survivors from the Jacobite centre kept charging but moved to the right and massed with the charging right flank. Leaving a trail of dead and wounded behind them, the Highlanders approached the Government lines, only to be hit by further volleys of musket fire on their right from the Campbells and parts of Wolfe's regiment, stationed behind the stonewall. But the Highlanders were not to be denied and smashed into Barrel's and Munro's regiments. Five hundred clansmen burst through the first line of Government troops, only to be met by the second line. Cumberland had drilled his soldiers to use their bayonets, not on the enemy directly in front of them, but on the man to the right. With his broadsword raised to strike, this left the clansman open to the thrust of the bayonet from the side. One Government soldier recalled:

... It was dreadful to see the enemies' swords circling in the air ... And to see the officers of the army, some cutting with their swords, others pushing with spontoons [spears], the sergeants running their halberds [pikes with axe heads] into the throats of their opponents, the men's bayonets up to the sockets.

The left flank of the Jacobite army, the MacDonalds, refused to charge at first, then advanced close to the Government lines but no further. Meanwhile, the Campbells had broken down part of the stonewall in front of them to allow 500 mounted Government dragoons to ride through and attack the Jacobites from behind. The entire Jacobite army began to retreat with units of the second line providing some protection. Prince Charles showed no desire to attempt to lead from the front, but quickly fled. The Government troops began to advance, putting to death any wounded Highlanders as they marched. At least 1000 Jacobites lay dead on the battlefield, while only 50 Government troops were killed and 260 wounded. The Chevalier de Johnstone, one of Bonnie Prince Charlie's officers, wrote that:

The road from Culloden was covered in bodies. The Duke of Cumberland stripped the wounded of their clothes and left them on the battlefield for two days alongside the dead. Then he sent soldiers to kill any who were still alive. He ordered a barn with Highlanders in it to be set alight, and his soldiers drove back any who tried to save themselves from the flames.

Some days after the battle, Lord George Murray wrote to Bonnie Prince Charlie to explain why they had lost the campaign:

It was highly wrong to have set up the royal standard without having positive assurance from the King of France that he would assist you with all his force ... It was a fatal error to allow the enemy those walls upon their left which made it impossible for us to break them ... Mr Hay, whom your Royal Highness trusted with ordering provisions, neglected his duty to such a degree that our ruin might probably have been prevented had he done his duty: in short the last three days, which were critical, our army starved.

After the Battle of Culloden the Duke of Cumberland remained in Scotland for three months, rounding up some 3500 men, mainly Highlanders, of whom he executed about 120. For this he earned himself the nickname of 'the Butcher'. In celebration of his victory the English named a flower after him, 'Sweet William'. The Scots showed their feelings by renaming an unpleasant weed 'Stinking Billy'.

■ The Duke of Cumberland's men rounded up and slaughtered many of the Scots rebels

Results of the Rebellion

Bonnie Prince Charlie escaped from the battlefield, and spent the next few months hiding from the Government forces. He moved around Scotland, being sheltered by loyal Highlanders, but it was clear that his hopes of challenging George II were at an end. He eventually escaped to the Isle of Skye, with the assistance of Flora Macdonald, the stepdaughter of the commander of the local militia, who risked her life to help him.

The rebellion of Bonnie Prince Charlie is sometimes called the Forty Five, because it took place in 1745, and it inspired the famous Skye Boat Song:

Speed bonnie boat, like a bird on the wing,

Onward, the sailors cry,

Carry the lad that's born to be king

Over the sea to Skye.

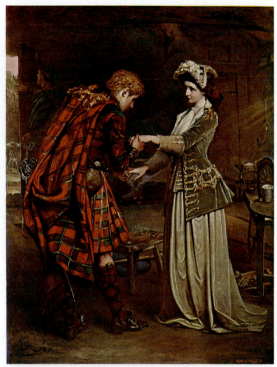

■ Bonnie Prince Charlie and Flora Macdonald take a sad farewell

Bonnie Prince Charlie escaped to France and spent the rest of his life in exile. He died in Rome in 1788. The Highlanders paid a very heavy price for their support of the Stuarts. Laws were passed making their national dress and the bagpipes illegal and they were disarmed. Many were sent into exile in the American colonies, including Flora Macdonald. Ironically, when the American colonies rebelled in the 1770s, many of these same men and their offspring fought for the Crown.

Exercise 10.3

1 Explain the reasons for the failure of the 1745 Rebellion.

2 If you had been one of Bonnie Prince Charlie's advisors, what advice would you have given him that might have changed the outcome of the rebellion?

3 The two sides, Government and Jacobite, would have given very different versions of the Battle of Culloden. Write the contrasting headlines and opening paragraphs for:

(a) a London newspaper in April 1746

(b) an Inverness newspaper in April 1746.

Exercise 10.4

Read the following sources and answer the questions that follow:

SOURCE A: An account of the 1745 Rebellion from a modern history book published in 1977.

A year before (1744) a much better equipped expedition, with French assistance, had set sail from France, but it had been beaten back by a superior British fleet and bad weather. Now Charles arrived with such little help that even his supporters, dismayed at his chances, urged him to return.

SOURCE B: The Highland attack on the Grenadier Company of Barrell's King's Own Royal Regiment (right); painted in late 1746 by David Morier for the Duke of Cumberland, reputedly using members of the regiment and Highland prisoners as models.

SOURCE C: From the Duke of Cumberland's account of the Battle of Culloden, written on 18 April 1746.

As their whole first line came down to attack at once, their right somewhat outflanked Barrell's regiment, and our greatest losses occurred there. But soon with the help of other regiments firing upon them Barrell's regiment beat them with their bayonets. The Scots were driven back and they then threw stones at us for a minute or two, before their total rout began.

■ The Highland attack

10 George I and George II

SOURCE D: From a British major's account after the Battle of Culloden in April 1746.

They have not had such a thrashing since the days of Cromwell, and whatever the Jacobites may say to lessen their losses, believe them not. The country is covered with their dead bodies and arms and the prisons are full of their prisoners ... I hope we shall soon finish this rebellion and bring their nobles in chains and their chiefs in fetters of iron.

1   What can you learn from Source A about Bonnie Prince Charlie's chances of success in the 1745 Rebellion?

2   What can you learn from Source C about how the Government troops defeated the Scots at Culloden?

3   How far does Source B agree with Source C about the attack on Barrell's regiment?

4   Using all the sources and your own knowledge, how far do you agree that the Jacobite defeat at Culloden was inevitable?

The end of the story

So was this the end of the story ... or just the beginning? By the end of the period covered by this book, Britain was a very different place from the one we read about in the introduction (page xi). The semi-feudal England of 1485 had been replaced by a recognisably more modern 'United Kingdom', with a powerful Parliament, a growing overseas trading empire and a constitutional monarchy. When George II died in 1760, in the midst of yet another war with France, the Seven Years' War, what was to become the British Empire was already influencing government policy in a way unimaginable in 1485. You will learn how this empire developed in the next book of this series, *Britain and Empire 1750–1914*.

Appendix 1: Timeline

The monarchs of England, 1485–1750

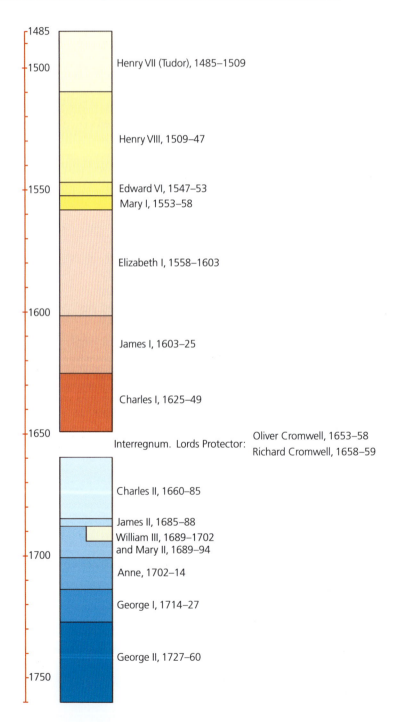

1485

1500 — Henry VII (Tudor), 1485–1509

Henry VIII, 1509–47

1550 — Edward VI, 1547–53
Mary I, 1553–58

Elizabeth I, 1558–1603

1600 —

James I, 1603–25

Charles I, 1625–49

1650 —

Interregnum. Lords Protector: Oliver Cromwell, 1653–58
Richard Cromwell, 1658–59

Charles II, 1660–85

James II, 1685–88
William III, 1689–1702
and Mary II, 1689–94

1700 —

Anne, 1702–14

George I, 1714–27

George II, 1727–60

1750

Appendix 2: Family trees

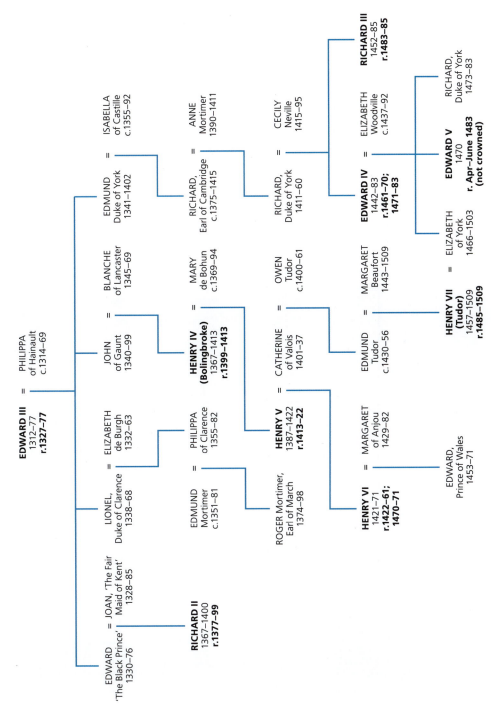

The family tree shows the following individuals and relationships:

- **EDWARD III** 1312–77 **r.1327–77** = PHILIPPA of Hainault c.1314–69
- EDWARD 'The Black Prince' 1330–76 = JOAN, 'The Fair Maid of Kent' 1328–85
  - **RICHARD II** 1367–1400 **r.1377–99**
- LIONEL, Duke of Clarence 1338–68 = ELIZABETH de Burgh 1332–63
  - PHILIPPA of Clarence 1355–82 = EDMUND Mortimer c.1351–81
    - ROGER Mortimer, Earl of March 1374–98
- JOHN of Gaunt 1340–99 = BLANCHE of Lancaster 1345–69
  - **HENRY IV (Bolingbroke)** 1367–1413 **r.1399–1413** = MARY de Bohun c.1369–94
    - **HENRY V** 1387–1422 **r.1413–22** = CATHERINE of Valois 1401–37 = OWEN Tudor c.1400–61
      - **HENRY VI** 1421–71 **r.1422–61; 1470–71** = MARGARET of Anjou 1429–82
        - EDWARD, Prince of Wales 1453–71
      - EDMUND Tudor 1430–56 = MARGARET Beaufort 1443–1509
        - **HENRY VII (Tudor)** 1457–1509 **r.1485–1509** = ELIZABETH of York 1466–1503
- EDMUND Duke of York 1341–1402 = ISABELLA of Castille c.1355–92
  - RICHARD, Earl of Cambridge c.1375–1415 = ANNE Mortimer 1390–1411
    - RICHARD, Duke of York 1411–60 = CECILY Neville 1415–95
      - **EDWARD IV** 1442–83 **r.1461–70; 1471–83** = ELIZABETH Woodville c.1437–92
        - **EDWARD V** 1470 **r. Apr–June 1483 (not crowned)**
        - RICHARD, Duke of York 1473–83
        - ELIZABETH of York 1466–1503
      - **RICHARD III** 1452–85 **r.1483–85**

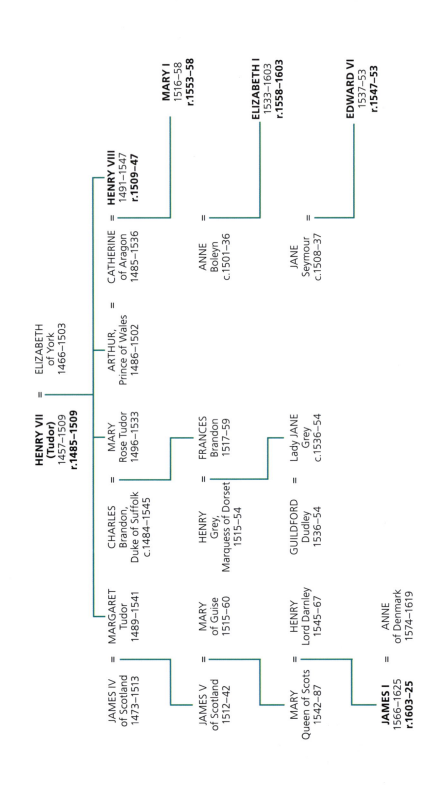

MARY I
1516–58
r.1553–58

HENRY VIII
1491–1547
r.1509–47

=

CATHERINE
of Aragon
1485–1536

ELIZABETH I
1533–1603
r.1558–1603

=

ANNE
Boleyn
c.1501–36

EDWARD VI
1537–53
r.1547–53

=

JANE
Seymour
c.1508–37

ELIZABETH
of York
1466–1503

=

ARTHUR,
Prince of Wales
1486–1502

**HENRY VII
(Tudor)**
1457–1509
r.1485–1509

=

MARY
Rose Tudor
1496–1533

=

CHARLES
Brandon,
Duke of Suffolk
c.1484–1545

FRANCES
Brandon
1517–59

=

HENRY
Grey,
Marquess of Dorset
1515–54

Lady JANE
Grey
c.1536–54

=

GUILDFORD
Dudley
1536–54

MARGARET
Tudor
1489–1541

=

JAMES IV
of Scotland
1473–1513

MARY
of Guise
1515–60

=

JAMES V
of Scotland
1512–42

HENRY
Lord Darnley
1545–67

=

MARY
Queen of Scots
1542–87

ANNE
of Denmark
1574–1619

=

JAMES I
1566–1625
r.1603–25

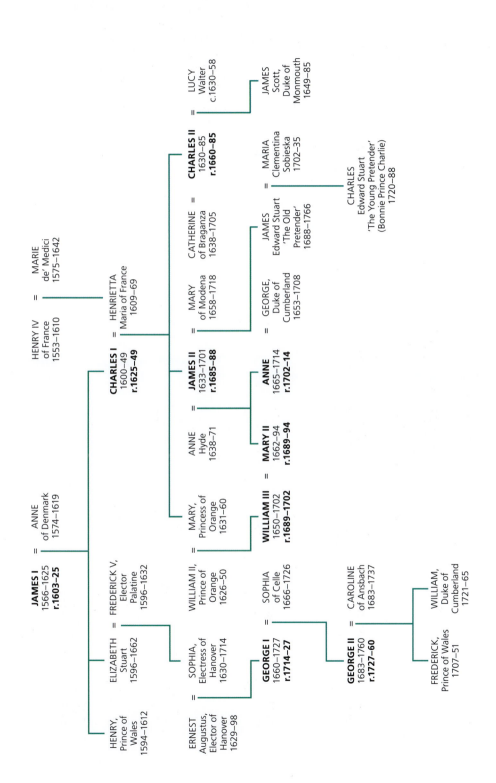

Appendix 3: Willie, Willie, Harry, Ste

And finally ... As a way of remembering the kings and queens of England, many of whom you have learnt about in this book, here is an old schoolboy rhyme:

Willie, Willie, Harry, Ste,

Harry, Dick, John, Harry three;

One, two, three Neds, Richard two,

Harrys four, five, six ... then who?

Edwards four, five, Dick the bad,

Harrys (twain*), then Ned (the lad);

Mary, Bessie, James the vain,

Charlie, Charlie, James again.

Will and Mary, Anna Gloria,

Georges four, then Will, Victoria;

Edward seven, George and Ted,

George the sixth, now Liz instead.

* Note that twain means two.

Learn this by heart and you will never forget who ruled when ever again.

Glossary

Act of Ten Articles   An Act of 1536 that recognised only the three sacraments of baptism, penance, and the Eucharist.

Amicable Grant   A tax that did not need the approval of Parliament; the initiative of Thomas Wolsey to raise money for war.

annulment   A decree by which a marriage is considered never to have existed.

baptism   The symbolic cleansing of sin, permitting entry to the church community.

benevolences   Compulsory Gifts to the Crown; a method of raising money used by Henry VIII.

Bill of Attainder   An Act of Parliament declaring someone guilty without a trial; a method used by Parliament to sentence the Earl of Strafford to death in 1641.

Cavalier Parliament   The royalist Parliament sitting between 1661 and 1679, that was supportive of Charles II.

Chantries   Chapels to which money was left by people who wanted masses to be said for their souls after their death. Abolished by the Chantries Act of 1547.

Civil List   A grant of money made to the monarch.

Clarendon Code   A series of Acts in the 1660s that discriminated against Catholics and upheld the Anglican communion.

common land   Under the medieval Feudal System, land upon which all people in a village could graze their animals and collect firewood from.

Convention Parliament   The Parliament sitting in 1660 which set about dismantling all the Acts of Parliament and institutions set up during the Commonwealth and Protectorate.

conventicles   Unauthorised meetings by several people for worship. These were outlawed by the Coventicle Act of 1664, part of the Clarendon Code.

covenant   A formal promise to do, or refrain from doing, something.

decimation tax   A tax introduced by Oliver Cromwell in 1655, to raise money for local armies.

dispensation   Special permission from the Pope, e.g. to marry under special circumstances.

dissenters   The name given to Puritans and non-conformists after the interregnum.

Divine Right of Kings   The belief that kings derive their power directly from God, and are not accountable to their subjects.

dowry   A contribution of land or money by a woman entering a marriage.

enclosure   The act of fencing off and dividing common land that had previously been open to all.

Eucharist   The commemoration of Christ's Last Supper by the consecration of bread and wine.

excommunicate   The action of prohibiting someone from taking part in church services.

Feudal System   A medieval system of military service and tax, based on the amount of land held by each section of society.

fireships   Unmanned ships that were filled with flammable materials, set on fire, and allowed to drift into the enemy fleet.

house of correction   An institution for the idle poor, rather like a prison.

impeachment   The act of removing someone from their position.

impotent poor   The name given to beggars and vagrants.

indoor relief   The aid given to the poor of a parish in a poorhouse.

indulgence   An intervention by the Church on behalf of a person who wanted to spend less time in Purgatory.

interregnum   Latin for 'between reign'; the name given to the period of 1649–60, when there was no reigning monarch in England.

legal quays   Quays at which foreign goods could be unloaded. Revenue from these quays went to the Crown.

monopoly   The exclusive right to sell a product, or to trade in a particular area.

outdoor relief   The aid given to the poor of a parish at their homes.

Overseers of the Poor   Two people appointed in each parish, who would collect the Poor Rate from the rich and distribute it to the poor.

Pale   The area of Ireland around Dublin that was under English control.

penance   The act of performing a punishment, like prayer or fasting, by a repentant sinner.

Petition of Right   A document drawn up by John Pym in 1628, which outlined the abuses by Charles I against Parliament.

Pluralism   The action of churchmen holding more than one office at a time, and collecting the revenue from all of them.

Poor Rate   The money from the rich that was collected by the Overseers of the Poor.

predestination   The Calvinist idea that people are destined for either Heaven or Hell from before they are born.

Presbyterians   Followers of John Knox, who followed a radical form of Protestantism close to Calvinism.

prorogue   The act of discontinuing a session of Parliament without formally ending it.

Protestantism   The movement challenging the teachings and traditions of the Roman Catholic Church, started by Martin Luther.

Purgatory   The place where Catholics believed the soul would go after death, to be cleansed from all its earthly sins.

Puritans   The name given to extreme Protestants who wanted to purify the Church.

recognisance   A written contract by which nobles paid a sum of money to guarantee their good behaviour.

regicide   The act of killing a monarch, or one who kills a monarch.

relics   The remains of saints, or objects associated with the Bible, which were often preserved in churches.

recusancy fines   Fines for Catholics who refused to attend Protestant services.

retainers under arms   Private armies in the employment of nobles.

retaining   The action of keeping a private army.

ship money   A tax for building ships, originally applied only to coastal areas but extended to the whole country in 1635 by Charles I.

spinet   A keyed instrument resembling a small harpsichord.

subsidy   A tax that varied depending on the wealth of the taxpayer, devised by Thomas Wolsey.

sufferance wharves   Quays that were used when legal quays became overcrowded.

tenants-in-chief   The most important landowners, who paid homage and swore fealty directly to the king.

tithes   Taxes raised by the Church.

transubstantiation   The idea that Christ's body is actually present in the bread and wine consumed at Communion during Mass.

vestments   Garments worn by priests at Mass.

viol   A six-stringed instrument, held between the knees and played with a bow.

Index